# EUCHARIST

## Christ's Feast With The Church

Laurence Hull Stookey

Abingdon Press
Nashville

EUCHARIST: Christ's Feast with the Church



*This book is printed on recycled, acid-free paper.*

**Library of Congress Cataloging-in-Publication Data**

Sookey, Laurence Hull, 1937–
Eucharist: Christ's feast with the church/Laurence Hull Stookey.
p. cm.
Includes bibliographical references and index.
ISBN 0-687-12017-9 (alk. paper)
1. Lord's supper. 2. Calvinism. I. Title.
BV825.S67 1993
234'.163—dc20 92-42832
CIP

95 96 97 98 99 00 01 02 03 04 — 10 9 8 7 6 5 4

MANUFACTURED IN THE UNITED STATES OF AMERICA

In gratitude for the teaching ministry of three who,
during my student days at Wesley Seminary,
instructed me in the meaning of the Eucharist:
Douglas Robson Chandler
Lowell Brestel Hazzard
Walter Earl Ledden

| challenge | inform + shape |
| --- | --- |
| reformers perspect. | scripture |
| one cup<br>- sanitation | central meanings |
| for the baptized<br>- contrary to exp. | elements |
| | for the baptized |

# CONTENTS

# INTRODUCTION

In addition to suggesting new ways of understanding and conducting the Eucharist, this book seeks to bring together in a single volume historical, theological, and practical matters that otherwise must be gleaned from an array of separate works, many of them written in technical vocabulary. Material that is of a specialized nature or that would interrupt the flow of the basic discussion is placed in the notes at the end of the book; thus I have attempted to provide a work whose essential content is accessible to laity, as well as a resource that provides additional material for seminarians and church professionals. The work is ecumenical in scope, but for those of my own Methodist heritage, an appendix is provided to cover particular concerns within the Wesleyan tradition.

Much of the basic work for this volume was done while I was on sabbatical leave in Auckland, New Zealand, during 1990. I am deeply grateful for assistance given to me (particularly with library and computer resources) by members of the staff and faculties of the New Zealand Baptist Theological College and of St. John's/Trinity Theological Colleges, a joint Anglican-Methodist seminary. Special gratitude is due to Ray French and Professors Terry Falla and Harold Pidwell at NZBTC, and to Jill van de Geer and Professors Frank Hanson and Godfrey Nicholson at St. John's/Trinity. I am grateful for the invitation of these schools to teach part-time and to do research in a country unmatched both for physical beauty and effusive hospitality.

My colleagues at Wesley Theological Seminary have been most helpful in a multitude of ways, in addition to that of granting sabbatical leave. For accuracy in historical matters, I have especially depended on Professor Mark S. Burrows, now on the faculty at Andover Newton Theological School; his suggestions have done much to shape the final form of the book, as have those of Professor John D. Godsey. As a way of checking the accessibility of the work to informed laity, I have relied on the very helpful comments of Drs. Charles and Elizabeth Tidball of Washington. Special appreciation is extended to Rex Matthews, Ulrike Guthrie, and Linda Allen on the editorial staff of Abingdon Press; to Veronica Boutte, faculty secretary; and to Mary Jo Sims-Baden, a student at Wesley Seminary. Their assistance in editing and proofreading copy has been crucial.

This book is gratefully dedicated to three persons who turned my own emerging theology of the Eucharist in new directions while I was a student at Wesley Seminary from 1959 to 1962:

Douglas Robson Chandler (b. 1901), Professor of Church History from 1939 to 1973, gave me an invaluable historical perspective and, when I was preparing a term paper on the Wesleyan view of the sacrament, introduced me to J. Ernest Rattenbury's *The Eucharist Hymns of John and Charles Wesley,* a volume to which I have turned again and again. Nearly twenty years after retirement, Professor Chandler continues to be a deeply loved and active member of the Wesley Seminary community.

Lowell Brestel Hazzard (1898–1978), Professor of Old Testament from 1951 to 1970, held a vital evangelical belief in the presence of Christ in the Eucharist, coupled with a passion for social reform that flowed out of this understanding. Together with a multitude of theological students, I received from him a rich and enduring legacy of a faith that seeks to be both informed and active.

W. Earl Ledden (1888–1984) taught liturgics at Wesley Seminary for six years following his retirement in 1960 as an active bishop of The Methodist Church. Until his death he was a generous and cherished friend of the school. He brought to his teaching a keen pastoral sensitivity and a particular insistence on the role of liturgical music, both of which have benefited me greatly.

For the ministry of these three teachers I am immensely thankful. I hope to pass on to my own students the kind of knowledge and vital piety Professors Chandler, Hazzard, and Ledden have conveyed to me.

It is a basic tenet of this book that the Eucharist teaches us Christian stewardship generally, and in particular instructs us in sharing the gifts of creation with those who have less in our society than most of us. In an attempt to embody this conviction, all royalties from this book are being assigned in equal portions to Wesley Seminary and to Bread for the City, an ecumenical service agency in Washington, D.C., dedicated to providing food, clothing, medical services, and other necessities to those who have been denied the opportunities and assistance that most of us can take for granted.

Laurence Hull Stookey
Wesley Theological Seminary
Washington, D.C.

*Was ever another command so obeyed? For century after century, spreading slowly to every continent and country and among every race on earth, this action has been done, in every conceivable human circumstance, for every conceivable human need from infancy and before it to extreme old age and after it, from the pinnacles of earthly greatness to the refuge of fugitives in the caves and dens of the earth. Men have found no better thing than this to do for kings at their crowning and for criminals going to the scaffold; for armies in triumph or for a bride and bridegroom in a little country church; for the proclamation of a dogma or for a good crop of wheat; for the wisdom of the Parliament of a mighty nation or for a sick old woman afraid to die; for a schoolboy sitting an examination or for Columbus setting out to discover America; for the famine of whole provinces of for the soul of a dead lover; in thankfulness because my father did not die of pneumonia; for a village headman much tempted to return to fetich because the yams had failed; because the Turk was at the gates of Vienna; for the repentance of Margaret; for the settlement of a strike; for a son for a barren woman; for Captain so-and-so, wounded and prisoner of war; while the lions roared in the nearby amphitheatre; on the beach at Dunkirk; while the hiss of scythes in the thick June grass came faintly through the windows of the church; tremulously, by an old monk on the fiftieth anniversary of his vows; furtively, by an excelled bishop who had hewn timber a day in a prison camp near Murmansk; gorgeously, for the commission of S. Joan of Arc—one could fill many pages with the reasons why men have done this, and not tell a hundredth part of them. And best of all, week by week and month by month, on a hundred thousand successive Sundays, faithfully, unfailingly, across all the parishes of christendom, the pastors have done this just to* make *the* plebs sancta Dei*—the holy common people of God.*

# PROLOGUE

*Babette's Feast,* a movie based on a short story by Isak Dinesen (Karen Blixen-Finecke), centers on a small, devout community along the bleak coast of Jutland. Babette arrives there as a refugee from the political turmoil of the Paris Commune. Two kindly but impoverished women accede to her pleas to be taken into their home. As pastor of the village, the women's late father founded the religious fellowship, and they struggle to keep it alive, beset as it is by pettiness, dissension, and impending extinction. They teach Babette to prepare the meager meals they share with the poor and sick, and for decades she serves them faithfully in exchange for only an austere room and a subsistence diet.

Then Babette learns she holds a winning lottery ticket. The sisters assume she will leave them to pursue an independent life in France. Instead, she sends to Paris for the finest foods, wines, china, and crystal. She plans and prepares a sumptuous feast for the little band of religious folk on the occasion of the hundredth anniversary of the birth of their founder.

But the puritanical bent of the faithful sets them against the feast, even before it is held. They agree that while they must accept Babette's hospitality, they certainly need not—indeed dare not—enjoy the cuisine. Thus they gather dourly at the table she has set so lovingly and skillfully. Yet as the meal progresses, the pleasures these pious folk have never even imagined begin to entice them in spite of themselves. A visiting nephew of the most prosperous member of the fellowship—a military officer, well schooled and traveled, and characterized by discrimination—

thoroughly appreciates the feast. With all the authority of his position, he interprets to the assembly the unique magnificence of the grand dinner. Only once, he says, has he encountered cuisine so wonderful—and that in the most prestigious restaurant of Paris.

Those gathered at the table soon begin to warm to the feast, and to each other. Old grudges are forgiven, new pleasures experienced, and in the end those who came unwillingly are dancing in the village street, despite their age and the chill of the night air.

Only then is Babette's true identity revealed. She acknowledges to the sisters that before the upheaval that drove her from France, it was she who was the chef of that preeminent Paris restaurant. Further, this most applauded cook in Europe used up her entire lottery prize to give this obscure village a banquet they did not want—and in the process to bring about a reconciliation and joy they could have experienced in no other way.

Whether intended by those who made the film or unintentional, is not Babette a superb Christ-figure: the incognito person of honor who humbly assumes the role of a servant, joyfully and freely sacrificing all for the transformation of those she loves? And is not Babette's marvelous feast strangely akin to what some Christians call the Eucharist and others the Mass and still others the Supper of the Lord or Holy Communion?[1]

Regardless of the name we give it, many Christians go reluctantly and glumly to that table, determined they will not—yes, dare not—enjoy it. It is something to be endured in order to fulfill Jesus' command, "Do this in remembrance of me." And that is all! Yet when we come often enough and stay long enough, unwittingly the faithful find there a banquet whose richness and delight cannot be anticipated. The feast is intended to allure, then compel, and finally draw into true community those who share it. The wonder of this banquet—Christ's feast with the church—we now pursue, the better to enjoy it and to be nurtured, changed, and emboldened by it.

# CHAPTER ONE

# CENTRAL MEANINGS BEHIND THE MEAL

Eating and drinking are not only necessary to life, but also in human societies most commonly they are communal activities. Human beings enjoy eating and drinking together—hence the prevalence of those experiences known as banquets, parties, and even regular household meals. The English words *companion* and *company* both are formed from two Latin roots meaning "those who share bread" with each other.[1] Persons who regularly must eat alone often report diminished enjoyment of their food, and they sometimes suffer poor nutrition for reasons that have nothing to do with economics. There is simply less incentive to cook a complete meal for one person or to eat a balanced diet when alone. The desire to be together when eating and drinking appears to be a universal human characteristic.

Furthermore, partaking of food and drink is also a universal way of marking significant experiences. Births and baptisms are marked by dinners and receptions, as are birthdays and anniversaries of all kinds. A wedding without some form of eating and drinking integral to it is impossible to comprehend. In the work-a-day world, many a business deal has been arranged or celebrated over food and drink, and committee and discussion groups of all kinds meet regularly over lunch. At the far end of the life cycle, after the funeral of a loved one, families reconstitute themselves around a table; indeed grief seems somehow lessened by such a community meal. In every culture the importance of communal eating and drinking is evident.

Thus it is hardly surprising that God, who made us and best

knows how we are put together, should provide for us a holy meal. Given the misunderstanding in the church for centuries about the meaning of this meal, and given the unexciting way in which it often is conducted, what may be surprising is that we should refer to this meal as a "feast."

As commonly observed, each person at the Lord's Table receives a bit of bread the size of a coin or smaller and no more wine than would fit into a thimble.[2] For reasons that will be explored later, in much Roman Catholic practice the wine is not drunk at all except by the officiating priest. In many churches of varying denominations, the bread is the thickness of cardboard and more resembles a certain kind of food reserved for goldfish than anything eagerly eaten at home, let alone at a party. Even when ordinary household bread is used, often it is neatly cubed in a way that seems designed to make it as unlike familiar food as possible. How can such an odd meal be called a feast?

The type and amount of food and drink offered at the Lord's Table are important considerations, and we will look at them closely in chapter 6. But for now there is a far more important underlying consideration: What we eat and drink in the Lord's name is important in its meaning more than in its form or amount. By inquiring deeply into that meaning—or better, meanings—we may come to a new basis for assessing things, even perhaps God's way of assessing things. We so readily judge the value of something or someone by quantity or appearance, but God teaches us that sounder judgment is based on quality and significance.

Therefore we begin with the message material things can convey rather than with the form of the things themselves. This we do by recalling God's story in the categories of creation, covenant, Christ, church, and coming kingdom; within these categories are biblical meanings behind the feast.[3]

## CREATION AS DIVINE COMMUNICATION

The Bible is the story of God's creation on its way to fulfillment in a new creation; for Christians that new creation was inaugurated in Jesus Christ and is already being made manifest here and now, though it cannot yet be known fully. The whole of the first creation is, says Paul, "groaning" for that transformation, which is yet to be.[4] Even so, the continuity between the creation affirmed in the first three chapters of the Bible and the new creation envisioned in its last two chapters is of foundational importance. This connection distinguishes the Christian faith from any system of religion that believes in a separation between the physical and the spiritual, between this world and the next (to use traditional terms, however defined).[5]

If the present world is not God's creation, or if it is hopelessly spoiled so that even God cannot repair it, then physical things are useless as a means of conveying divine love. The existence of sacraments in the Christian tradition points in the other direction; God's grace can be proclaimed through things such as the water of baptism and the bread and wine of the holy meal. This is the case because creation has not been ruined beyond redemption; no matter how much of a mess God's creatures make of things, God, the maker of all, still seeks to communicate through creation itself.

Biblical teaching sees the purpose behind the creation of the universe to have been that of divine self-expression and sharing. God did not create because of some neurotic inner need (divine loneliness, for example). God is complete and full apart from anyone or anything else. But God's desire to share and be made known was the divine motivation for making all that is. Thus the Judeo-Christian tradition affirms that while the world around us can be abused and even destroyed by us, its intended foundational function is to reveal the goodness and love of God.

Eating figures prominently in the Genesis story of creation. God makes ample provision for the man and woman in the garden. They may feast on a multitude of foods; only one fruit is forbidden them. Even when they transgress, God changes the method but not the reality of eating. As a result of their rebellion, human beings will have to produce their food by the sweat of their brow, rather than by simply finding it in easy reach. But they are not consigned to starvation or even a subsistence diet, for one of their children becomes a tiller of the soil and the other a keeper of sheep. God will not take away food as a punishment for sin, though the means of its production may be altered. Food is not merely necessary for human life; it is a good gift from God and thus one way in which we come to know divine love.

Too often Christians have distorted this teaching in one direction or another. On one hand, the physical world is sometimes viewed with suspicion. Then it is believed that "spiritual" people needed to get out of a dangerous captivity to the material world and to find God apart from earthly experience. Thus God is set outside of creation; God and the world are antagonistic to each other. On the other hand, the more popular of the two current distortions sees creation as something good in and of itself without finding in it the self-revealing work of God. Enjoy the world as the world, rather than as a sign that points beyond itself to a creator. In this view, it is not that the world makes it difficult to find God, but that God is not important enough to be sought, if indeed there is a God at all. A theology of sacraments weighs such spiritualism and such materialism in the balance and finds both lacking.

Through the food and drink of the sacrament, God is made known as One revealed by earthly things. Ultimately this is crucial for Christians, for without it no sense can be made of Bethlehem. The world around us neither exists for itself nor is an impediment to spiritual insight. Creation is one lens (though not the only lens) through which we see divine goodness and intention.

This has crucial implications for daily living. Christians share with all others on earth an urgent concern for the welfare of the ecosystem, but for Christians more is at stake even than the continuation of life on the planet. What is most at stake is the continued communication of God's loving purpose through creation. Not only are we capable of destroying the good earth, but we are capable also of frustrating the goodness of God, who created that earth as one means of expressing divine love.

Furthermore, God in creation sought to make that love known to all, not just to some. We humans, in our arrogance, usually take this to mean "all people." But a closer and more humble reading of the biblical stories will suggest that creation is intended to reveal God's love to all created things.[6] The eucharistic meal is about sharing—sharing both with all people (particularly those who are not permitted to see divine goodness because greed has kept God's bounty from them) and with the whole created order.

Human responsibility in relation to creation is suggested by the kinds of things employed in the Eucharist. Bread and wine do not occur in creation. God gives grains of wheat and grapes and soil in which they can grow. But someone must nurture stalk and vine, grind flour and knead dough, and press the grapes. Thus what we eat and drink at the Table of the Lord suggests cooperation between Creator and creature as we are called responsibly to tend, prepare, and share with one another. Needless to say, the bread and wine at the Lord's Table also imply the need to care for the environment, even if this demands self-sacrifice, so that wheat and grapes (which in the Supper come to represent all good things) can continue to flourish.

All this meaning—in a tiny bit of food and drink. But that is only the beginning.

## COVENANTAL INITIATION AND INTERACTION

Paul and the writers of the first three Gospels report that in presenting bread and wine to those in the upper room, Jesus spoke of the blood of the covenant. That said far more to the disciples and first readers of the Gospels, steeped as they were in Judaism, than to us who have forgotten so much of our heritage. A covenant in the biblical sense was a deep relationship, never taken casually. Ancient Israel saw God's initiating love for a powerless people oppressed by Pharaoh as comparable (if infinitely more wonderful) to the graciousness of an earthly ruler who out of love for the citizenry established a bond and commitment between monarch and people.

Hebraic theology recognized this covenant-like goodness of God for what it was, sheer grace: "It was not because you were more numerous than any other people that the Lord . . . chose you—for you were the fewest of all peoples. It was because the Lord loved you" (Deut. 7:7-8).

The covenantal meaning of the Lord's Supper often has been ignored precisely in this regard. Frequently, communion has been seen less as a gift of love from God than as a reward for virtuous living or faithful service. Thus some people are hesitant to receive the sacrament for fear they are "not good enough." This misses the meaning of how biblical covenants come to be initiated.

Still, the instinct about some kind of obligation to God is not utterly wrong. Once instituted, a covenant makes demands on those who have entered it. God called Israel for a purpose: faithful service. When the people misinterpreted the covenant as sheer privilege, things went drastically awry. Then the prophets, recognizing the need for human responsibility, announced judgment and called for repentance, saying of the rebellious people in the name of God:

> The more I called them,
> the more they went from me;
> .....................................................................
> I took them up in my arms;
> but they did not know that I healed them.
> I led them with cords of human kindness,
> with bands of love.
> I was to them like those
> who lift infants to their cheeks.
> I bent down to them and fed them.
> (Hos. 11:2-4)

But this nurturing covenant love of God was ignored, so that once more the people fell into slavery as God lamented, "My people are bent on turning away from me" (Hos. 11:7). Then the prophet called to the people: "Return to your God, hold fast to love and justice, and wait continually for your God" (Hos. 12:6).

Entrance into the covenant is not merited, but our acceptance of inclusion into the covenant implies constancy and righteous obedience. Eating is often a reminder of this. Annually the Hebrews reenacted the Passover with a highly symbolic meal through which the story of the escape from Pharaoh was experienced again. Most important to the meal were the bread and the lamb. Unleavened bread was eaten as a reminder of the gracious God who snatched the people out of Egypt with such dispatch that there was not time for yeast to cause dough to rise in the usual manner. And the Passover lamb was a reminder of the original animals' slaughter so that their blood, applied to the door posts of Hebrew homes, would ensure that the angel of death would harmlessly pass over the firstborn of Israel, whereas the firstborn of the Egyptians would die in the wake of Pharaoh's disobedience. Thus in the eating of the Passover meal there was both promise and warning: God is gracious in rescuing the afflicted, but faithless rebellion can bring with it undesired consequences.

Similarly, in at least one kind of covenant-making tradition, a sacrificial animal was cut in two and each half was placed on the ground with a space between. Those making the promises walked between the halves of the sacrifice as a sign of faithfulness, and presumably they were warned thereby that if they broke the covenant promises their lives, like that of the animal, would be required of them. (See Jeremiah 34:19.) While this may strike us as a warning of undue harshness, it emphasizes the point that covenant making is never casual, for broken covenants can bring with them broken hearts and lives. But God's covenant promises, unlike many human vows, can be trusted utterly.

The meaning for our eucharistic participation is this: We cannot earn from God an invitation to the Table of the Lord. But what is done there is intended to show us God's faithful ways of justice and mercy, and what is received there is meant to strengthen us for responsible and faithful service to God.

A covenant as a two-way relationship involving both grace and responsibility is aptly captured in these petitions of a contemporary eucharistic prayer: "Deliver us from the presumption of coming to this table for solace only, and not for strength; for pardon only, and not for renewal. Let the grace of this Holy Communion make us one body, one spirit in Christ, that we may worthily serve the world in his name."[7] And as this prayer suggests, it is Christ who is at the center of the feast of grace.

## CHRIST AT CENTER

Jesus Christ, according to the New Testament, is both the inaugurator of the new creation and the initiator of the new covenant. Christ brings into sharp focus what before was known more dimly. But the work of Christ is understood not only from the past forward but into the future. Thus from Christ emanates the covenant community of Christians called the church; and the new creation, known now only in part, will be known fully only in that event popularly called "the coming of the kingdom" (or more technically, the consummation). Thus there is a symmetry to the five categories we are discussing, with Christ at the center of the axis.

That Christ is plainly connected with eucharistic eating and drinking is evident, but often the understanding of this is too constricted and is taken to refer only (or at least primarily) to the events reported in the upper room on the night of betrayal and arrest. That meal, sometimes called "the Last Supper," must be set in a much wider context, as follows.

Nothing is more plain from the Gospel accounts than that Jesus loved to eat and drink. The charge of his opponents that he was a glutton and a drunkard is not to be taken literally.[8] Nevertheless, Jesus did raise the hackles of conventionally pious people in his time by feasting in the houses of tax collectors, including Zacchaeus (Matthew 9:11ff.; Luke 19:1-9), and others he offended by eating in the home of Simon (called "the leper" in Matthew 26:6 and Mark 14:3, but "the Pharisee" in Luke 7:36). When the crowds who followed him became hungry, he fed them, though they numbered in the thousands (Matthew 14:13-21 and parallels).

Jesus taught in parables centered on wedding feasts (e.g., Matthew 22:1-14 and 25:1-13), and at such an event in Cana he transformed water into wine, that the festivities might not be spoiled and the host embarrassed by lack of provisions (John 2:1-11). He turned aside those who wanted his disciples to fast in the manner of the disciples of John the Baptizer (Matthew 9:14-17 and parallels), and he rebuked those who complained that his followers violated the law of Moses because they plucked grain when they were hungry on the sabbath (Matthew 12:1-8 and parallels).

In all of this, far more was at stake than food and drink, however. At the beginning of his public life, Jesus rejected the notion of food at any price by refusing to turn stones into bread at the suggestion of the tempter (Matthew 4:3-4 and Luke 4:2-4). The focus of the new creation that Jesus was introducing was upon the glory of and obedience to God; when that focus included eating and drinking, well and good. But these acts are not the central purpose. Thus also, when Martha was preoccupied, presumably with preparing a meal, Mary's attention to the teaching of Jesus was commended over Martha's diligence in household tasks (Luke 10:40-41).

The crowds that followed Jesus were fed in order that thereby they might stay for further instruction and by the very act of sharing learn something of the nature of God. When, on one occasion, they returned the next day seeking a free meal rather than teaching, Jesus rebuked them and launched into a discourse on the true bread, which is from heaven (John 6:22ff.). Earlier, when calling the disciples, Jesus gave a bountiful catch of fish to Simon, James, and John (Luke 5:1-11). But far from being simply a way of preventing economic disaster to their fishing business, it was an occasion for helping them understand what it means to fish for those folk who can also become disciples.

Certainly for Jesus eating was never to be anything other than a sharing. The harshest words he seems ever to have put into the mouth of God were "You fool!"—directed at a selfish landowner who had stashed away bin upon bin of grain to provide for his own future (Luke 12:20). Equally strident is Jesus' condemnation of the sumptuously fed man, who blithely ignored the needs of hungry and homeless Lazarus on his doorstep (Luke 16:19-31).

Jesus' mealtime companions ran the gamut of society from socially unacceptable lepers and the unrighteous but ultimately penitent Zacchaeus, on the one hand, to the respected, but sometimes self-righteous, Pharisees on the other. Across that wide spectrum these meals of Jesus were to be seen as enacted illustrations of the scope of God's concern. Jesus' table fellowship is a manifestation of the new creation, which embraces all who are discriminated against in the course of normal human activity (according to what we might call "old creation rules") and yet are willing to hear the Good News with repentance, thus fulfilling covenant obedience.

Jesus' meal in the upper room before his death cannot be separated from all of the eating and drinking previously reported of him. But as we shall see in more detail in the next chapter, still less can it be understood apart from his meals with his followers after the resurrection. Indeed, all of those earlier meal accounts also must be read in the light of the resurrection, for a crucial assumption of the New Testament is that the ministry of Jesus makes sense only as we read it "backward." God's vindication of Jesus in the resurrection is an act so bold and drastic that everything prior must be understood in a new way. Since the New Testament documents were all written in the light of the resurrection, they already incorporate this radical reinterpretation. But if we naively read them as straightforward narrative history (as often we do) we are thereby robbed of this necessary insight.[9]

In the fullest New Testament tradition, then, eating and drinking with Jesus is enactment: The Eucharist is a feast in which we, with the risen Lord, incarnate the hope we have of a righteous realm in which Christ's sacrificial love destroys barriers among human beings and between humanity and God. To this feast all are invited by God on equal terms.

The same God who graciously rescued and preserved the Hebrew slaves has now extended grace to all people. Thus Jesus, in his death, is seen as the great paschal lamb, whose blood saves us from the angel of death and on whose flesh we feast in order to have life. None approaches the feast by means of merit, but all are invited by grace. There none may boast or dominate or exclude, for this is Christ's feast. Christ is the host, and hence the one who sets the rules.

If the Eucharists we know are less than that, the difficulty lies in the perplexing nature of the church. At this we now look.

## THE CHURCH: AT ONCE INADEQUATE AND ASPIRING

Theologically understood, the church is the covenant community of Christ's people; it is the company of those who know they live by grace and believe themselves incorporated into the transforming work of the resurrection. Sociologically understood, the church is a collection of individuals flawed to the same extent as the rest of humanity, and as often as not trapped in the assumptions and limitations imposed upon them by their surrounding culture. It is in the midst of the collision of these two understandings that Christians must live. On the one hand, the church aspires to be an evident witness on earth of what God's righteous rule is like; on the other hand, the church is so comfortable with and conformable to the prevailing standards of society that any witness it gives seems utterly inadequate—perhaps even mocking of the ideals of the Gospel.

The collision is all too evident at the Lord's Table. There presumably Christ invites all who enter into the covenant of the gospel. Yet the church is divided into hundreds of denominations; many of these do not welcome at the Table members of other groups. Even in those denominations that officially have "open communion," in fact at a practical level all kinds of exclusion occurs. Likely, for example, congregations of white members and of black members meet separately—and within such divisions communicants are largely segregated further by financial and educational factors. And the homeless, the poor, and those with HIV or mental retardation may be unwelcome in any of the above.

In the face of such realities, some people have simply given up in despair. In this view, the church will never be as good as it thinks it is; therefore, abandon the hypocrisy and look elsewhere—or nowhere—for hope. Others have envisioned and attempted to create sects of perfection. From such a perspective, the institutional church is indeed hopelessly inadequate; therefore, the truly committed must separate from the rest into utopian societies under the rule of God alone.

The problem is hardly new. The parable of the wheat and the weeds in Matthew 13 attests to its importance already in the church to which Matthew wrote. The message of the parable to us seems to be that the church will always be inadequate, yet must ever press on, aspiring to be a less distorted reflection of God's righteousness. Imbedded in this message is the faith that the risen Christ is with us, and with us in transforming power. Therein is the antidote both for a hopeless pessimism about the human nature of the church and for an arrogant self-righteousness that thinks Christians have already achieved perfection.

At the Table of the Lord the church is both judged and strengthened by Christ, the Host. The assurance of forgiveness, so often associated with the Eucharist, is legitimate only when we know that forgiveness is for the penitent, and penitence is literally a "turn-around" that involves change.

That change cannot be merely individualistic. The church is itself to be understood as a sign of the interconnectedness of life. The church is a body, says Paul, an organic system, not a collection of separated individual parts. We should be reminded of this by the fact that the Eucharist is normally received by congregations assembled in one place, not individuals in their own homes. (Chapter 7 will consider the exception created by those who are home-bound.) The social order in which the church is placed is also an organic system—indeed a very tangled web of problems and possibilities. Individual but separate efforts, no matter how well intentioned, are insufficient to bring about pervasive and permanent change in that social order.

Thus "table fellowship" among those within the church is crucial. The Eucharist is not each believer communicating separately with God, and happening to be in the same room for matters of convenience and efficiency. Often it seems to be assumed that Christians come together for worship primarily because this provides a psychological boost, or even because it is cheaper than if each person had to hire a private chaplain. Quite the opposite. Christians come together because the believers by definition are bound together. The congregation, not the individual, is the irreducible unit of Christianity.

Both the penitence and the change required of the church corporately and the communal table fellowship of the church are best understood in relation to the great feast of heaven to which we are beckoned as the redeemed of the Lord.

## THE COMING KINGDOM

Established and sustained by Christ, who has inaugurated the new creation and the new covenant, the church proclaims and awaits the fulfillment of God's purpose. That fulfillment often goes under the shorthand term *heaven.* Christians have been justly criticized for concepts of heaven that are unduly literalistic and even materialistic (with stress on streets and harps and crowns of gold) or irresponsibly escapist ("Fret not about injustice on earth; you will get pie in the sky when you die, by and by"). Recognizing the legitimacy of such criticism, the church has sometimes deflected it by deemphasizing or even evading the concept of heaven. Not only has this short-changed the biblical hope of God's triumph over all evil at the end of time, but it has also caused a serious diminution in the confidence and power of the people of God now on earth.

Heaven is not only about the future, but it is also about the past and the present. It is a means of connecting Christians now alive with all who went before them. Whatever else eternal life is, it is "the communion of saints"—the bond of grace between all Christians living and dead. The loss of the concept of heaven is also the loss of a companionship we rightly feel with all who have preceded us in the faith.

The old general preface to the eucharistic prayer noted that "with angels and archangels and with all the company of heaven" we praise and glorify God's holy name. But if heaven is gone, so is its whole company. And few things have so debilitated contemporary Christianity as its loss of the sense of continuity and solidarity with people of faith in every century and place. Isolation is a dreadful thing; and in an age that has little time for the study of history ("History is bunk," said Henry Ford), the church risks a fatal loneliness that causes us wrongly to suppose we are the first Christians ever to have had doubts or suffered persecution or striven for what seemed impossible.

To gather at the Lord's Table and affirm the presence of all the company of heaven is to see gathering with us the apostles and martyrs and the faithful of the ages—Chrysostom; Cyprian; Agatha; Cecilia; Monica and Augustine, with their beloved friend Ambrose; Francis of Assisi and Clare; Joan of Arc;

Francis Xavier; Katie and Martin Luther; Samuel and Susanna Wesley, together with all of their children, famous or lesser known. The list goes on. Add your own names, those whose faith challenged and encouraged you in years past. These are not dead. They surround the throne of God and sing songs to the Lamb. They feast at the great supper of heaven. And whenever we sing and come to eat and drink with Christ, we join them in anticipation of that day when we shall be no longer the fractured church on earth—but rather the one, holy, catholic, and apostolic church eternal in the great city of God.

This is but a continuation of the vision of the author of the book of Hebrews, who listed in chapter 11 the great catalogue of the worthies and then began chapter 12 with a magnificently encouraging metaphor: These are they who have run with faith their laps in the relay race. They have passed to us the baton. And we now run, but they surround us, hovering above us in the arena with shouts of encouragement: "Run steadily. By the example and ever-present grace of Christ, we completed our course without fainting or falling. So can you. Run swiftly now, and pass the baton on to those who come after you. Then come join us as we cheer others on."

The Eucharist is the feast of the whole church as it participates in and yet awaits the perfect reign of God. And what we expect to become, we seek to be now. The future of God is not some escapist notion that allows us to make peace with unrighteousness on earth; instead it is the divine tug that motivates the reform of the present state of things. At the Table of the Lord, we regularly join in the prayer of the Lord. The words "your kingdom come, your will be done on earth as it is in heaven" constitute not two petitions but one.

Those who glimpse the kingdom in the kingdom meal called the Eucharist thereafter strive to do already on earth what they have envisioned to be done in heaven. The striving will not result here and now in perfect achievement. But the struggle to achieve will be persistent—and tiring. Therefore at the holy Table, the church makes a daringly bold entreaty: "O Christ, come to feed us, to restore and invigorate us, until we join you in the Great Banquet prepared for all who love you to the end in faith and hope. Amen."

# CHAPTER TWO

# KEY BIBLICAL UNDERSTANDINGS OF THE EUCHARIST

Since an ample treatment of the full New Testament teaching about the Eucharist requires at least an entire volume, here we can briefly discuss only representative passages from Paul, the Synoptic Gospels, John's Gospel, and the Revelation. The passages have been selected to address crucial issues before the contemporary church as we seek a renewed understanding of the eucharistic feast.

## PAUL'S INSTRUCTION TO THE CORINTHIANS

The earliest understanding of the Eucharist in the church known to us comes from Paul's letter to the church he had established in Corinth. While the first three Gospels tell of Jesus' meals with his disciples, the traditions reported they were not composed in the form we have them until later; Paul's First Letter to the Corinthians was written about a quarter century after the resurrection, and its eleventh chapter is crucial both for what it contains and for ways in which it has been misunderstood.

At the heart of Paul's discussion is this assertion:

> For I received from the Lord what I also handed on to you, that the Lord Jesus on the night when he was betrayed took a loaf of bread, and when he had given thanks, he broke it and said, "This is my body that is [broken] for you. Do this in remembrance of me." In the same way he took the cup also, after supper, saying,

> "This cup is the new covenant in my blood. Do this, as often as you drink it, in remembrance of me." For as often as you eat this bread and drink the cup, you proclaim the Lord's death until he comes. (1 Cor. 11:23-26)

The most crucial word is one that is infuriatingly difficult to put into English—the Greek term *anamnesis,* rendered as "remembrance" in most translations of verse 25. Hence we must begin by considering the difference between remembering in our usual sense and in the sense Paul used it, growing out of his Jewish tradition.[1] To comprehend that difference, we need to engage in an imaginative exercise.

Suppose someone were to say to you, "Remember your high school graduation." Likely you would say, "Now, I'm going to have to think about that for a few minutes. Please give me some undisturbed peace and quiet. . . . Let's see, I can picture the building where it was held. My whole family was there, and it was crowded. I have no idea what the graduation speaker said, but I do remember going up to the platform to receive my diploma. Now what else can I remember? Oh yes, we had a nice party afterward." That is our accustomed way of "remembering." But if you "remembered" after the fashion of the ancient Hebrews, as mediated to the Corinthians by Paul, you would do something quite different. Challenged to remember your high school graduation, you would rent a cap and gown. Clad therein, with great dignity and pride you would walk across a room while a recording of "Pomp and Circumstance" played. Having previously engaged a caterer, you would then throw a party for your friends.

For most twentieth-century Christians, remembering is a solitary experience involving mental recall. But for ancient Jews and early Christians (the first of whom were all Jews), remembrance was a corporate act in which the event remembered was experienced anew through ritual repetition. To remember was to do something, not to think about something. Thus in verse 25, the words "do this" are even more crucial than "in remembrance of me." (Many Protestants thus have the wrong words carved into their communion tables.)

Do this! Do what? Take bread. Give thanks over the loaf for God's graciousness. Break the bread. Give the bread to the people of Christ. Take the cup. Again give thanks to God. Then give the cup to the congregation. (Unlike the Gospel writers, Paul does not specifically mention the distribution of the bread and cup. But that is clearly implied both by the action of breaking the bread so that all may share in it and by Paul's overall discussion of table practices in Corinth.)

With the exception of certain groups, such as the Society of Friends (Quakers), Christians have universally kept the command to "do this." Some have retained the seven distinct actions, four with the bread and three with the cup. But most Christians, for the sake of ease and efficiency, have combined the seven into what is called "the fourfold action":

1. Taking the bread and wine.
2. Giving thanks to God over these gifts of creation.
3. Breaking the loaf.
4. Giving the bread and cup to the people.

Almost universally we "do this," but often we suppose that in doing it, we are primarily to "think about this." We have become passive and cerebral, often thinking primarily about the historical ministry of Jesus. But the intention of Paul is that we actively participate—and in the participation experience anew for ourselves the presence of the living Christ among us.

*Among* is a deliberately chosen word, in contrast to what may be the more prevailing assumption, *within.*[2] *Within* can be singular and introspective. *Among* is plural and interactive. Unfortunately, English uses the same word *you* for both singular and plural, and therefore we have difficulty understanding the original meaning of Hebrew and Greek, which used different words for the singular and plural pronouns. In this section of 1 Corinthians, Paul consistently uses the plural form of *you.* This can be dismissed as "historical accuracy" in verses 24 and 25 since Jesus is being quoted as addressing the company of his disciples. But in verses 23 and 26 Paul could have chosen to address each reader of his letter individually by using *you* in the singular. He did not. In verse 23 he hands the teaching on to "you" in the plural ("y'all," in Southern colloquial American speech), as again he does when in verse 26 he exhorts us to proclaim the Lord by eating and drinking.

This same determined corporate way of thinking is implied by the words "I also handed on" (v. 23). What Paul is teaching is to be handed on from one generation to another. (Our word *tradition,* so often used with a sneer as being negative, is derived from the Latin *traditio,* which literally means "handing on, delivering.") Nor is the apostle's assertion, "For I received from the Lord what I also handed on to you," to be taken literally. Paul, of course, had no firsthand experience of the ministry of Jesus; nor is he here claiming some direct revelation. "What I also handed on" implies that this teaching had previously been handed on to him by the apostolic church. Because of his high regard for the church as the earthly body of Christ, Paul had no difficulty equating "from the hands of the Lord's apostles" with "from the Lord." The communal eating and drinking is to be handed on from one generation of Christians to the next and is an utterly corporate act by which we, the church, "proclaim the Lord's death until he comes."

There is also a corporate assumption built into the word translated "proclaim." This proclamation is a setting forth before the church and the world of the story of Jesus. The Greek term *katangello* suggests that the Lord's Supper is a way of announcing the good news (*evangellion*). The Supper is an evangelical act, for through it the church enacts the same transforming story that characterizes preaching and teaching. The latter have more to do with words that engage the sense of hearing, the former with acts that more fully engage the senses of sight, taste, touch, and smell.[3] Through the eucharistic feast, the saving work of Christ is declared directly to the congregation as a means of strengthening faith; it is proclaimed to the world indirectly, as Christians so fortified become witnesses in their communities to God's love.

What is proclaimed is "the Lord's death until he comes." First it must be said that "death" is here Paul's shorthand for Christ's full saving work. There is no intention of ignoring the ministry of Jesus, let alone his resurrection. Paul takes for granted the presence of the living Christ in the church between the time of the crucifixion and the Lord's return. But some misreadings of Paul have ignored this, with a literalism so fixed on Calvary as to make the Eucharist morose, if not indeed morbid—a kind of "funeral for Jesus." Nothing could be further from the Pauline meaning.

It must also be said that "until he comes" is for Paul a very hopeful phrase—indeed an invigorating one. The Eucharist is not a holding operation in which Christians engage to keep from being bored while they wait for something else to happen. The same Hebraic understanding of remembrance that allows us to experience anew the past also allows us to experience already the future. Unlike us, Paul would not consider the exhortation "remember the future" to be an oxymoron. One experiences the past by doing now what was done then; by doing now what will be done later, we already experience the future in our midst. (This future aspect of *anamnesis* is sometimes given a separate technical name, *prolepsis,* from the Greek word for "anticipation.")

Thus in the Supper of the Lord, that for which we hope becomes present in our experience. Or to put it another way, here and now we are already feasting at the great messianic banquet in heaven. It is for this reason that some writers refer to worship as "rehearsal" for the future. However, care should be taken with this comparison drawn from the dramatic stage. The associations of pretense ("play-acting") must be dismissed, and the power of dramatic art to engage and persuade must be highlighted. Further, what occurs in the eucharistic liturgy is not "a willful suspension of disbelief" but rather a divinely given increase of faith— faith that God controls the future and that the saving ministry of Jesus on earth is but the beginning of God's great good news.[4]

To summarize, in four brief verses, Paul challenges our usual ways of thinking about the Eucharist:

1. The sacrament is primarily actions done, not concepts contemplated. These actions (whether seven or four in

number) are of central importance and constitute the basic framework of the Eucharist.

2. These actions are thoroughly corporate, involving the church as Christian community, which in the name of Christ hands on its heritage from generation to generation. The sacrament is not primarily a matter of interior and individualist piety, nor is *tradition* a dirty word in the Christian vocabulary.
3. Through these historic, corporate actions both the past and the future become a part of our present experience. History and hope are not disjointed pieces, irrelevant to contemporary life and mission. Time, seen in Christian perspective, is a seamless garment.
4. Through these actions, the fullness of Christ's work is proclaimed with evangelical power. The Lord's Supper is not a dead ritual to be endured, but a vital, empowering announcement of grace.
5. All of this is done ultimately for the sake of the world, which Christ came to save. Far from being an esoteric, inconsequential church matter, it is participation in and proclamation of cosmic reality.

But now we must turn to a major problem engendered by this same chapter of Paul's Corinthian correspondence. Having declared the nature of the Lord's Supper, Paul goes on to warn:

> Whoever, therefore, eats the bread or drinks the cup of the Lord in an unworthy manner will be answerable for the body and blood of the Lord. Examine yourselves, and only then eat of the bread and drink of the cup. For all who eat and drink without discerning the body, eat and drink judgment against themselves. (1 Cor. 11:27-29)

Fewer biblical passages have wrought more mischief in the life of the church than this one—primarily because not enough of Paul's argument was read with a serious eye on the apostle's larger theological scheme. As a result, hordes of otherwise devout Christians have feared to partake of the sacrament lest this would somehow have a detrimental effect. In much contemporary piety this comes out as, "Oh, I don't take communion. I am not worthy of it."

Key to Paul's meaning is the phrase "discerning the body" in verse 29. The New Oxford Annotated Bible provides a helpful footnote that defines this phrase as "the community, one's relation to other Christians." Paul is making a quick connection, elusive to the casual reader, between the eucharistic body of Christ (the bread) and the ecclesial body of Christ (the church). He is warning against the danger of not understanding what it means to be the church as a corporate community.

All this is tied up in a particular problem at Corinth, which Paul begins discussing in verse 17 of chapter 11. The situation appears to have been this: The Eucharist in the early church was part of a larger community meal—likely a kind of potluck or covered-dish supper. At Corinth, the affluent church members, because of their flexible schedules, could arrive early with their ample provisions. But those who had to work stated hours could not arrive as soon, and those who were poor could contribute little or nothing to the community table. Rather than waiting for everyone to arrive, the wealthier members of the congregation began feasting early in the evening. By the time the others arrived most of the food and drinks were gone, and some people were indeed intoxicated.

What Paul is saying in verse 29 to these folk is: "You do not understand what it means to be the body of Christ. Your selfish acts stand in judgment over you. If you truly discerned what it means to be Christ's body, you would wait for all to arrive before beginning to eat. Then there would be an equal sharing rather than discrimination against fellow believers." This rebuke is carefully sandwiched between a strong assertion that the Eucharist is characterized by sharing (10:16-18) and an extended discussion of the interdependence of the parts in Christ's body (12:4-26).

There appears to be in our day no direct corollary to the Corinthian situation—congregations in which some arrive at a community meal only to find that others have begun early and already consumed everything. Does this mean Paul's word to Corinth says nothing to us? No. It means rather that in a world where many hunger while others overeat, we must see the meaning defined globally rather than congregationally. Most congregations know pretty well how to take care of their own; active members are not likely to be left starving if they fall on hard times. But it may be a different story for those nonmembers in a different part of town, or for people halfway around the world.

In our situation, Paul's counsel to us is not that we should cease receiving the Eucharist (as Christians have often supposed), but that we should stop dissociating it from the rest of life. Instead of being something to save (or damn) us individually, the Eucharist's more important function is to teach us to share, to demonstrate before our very eyes the interconnectedness of life in a universe created by a gracious God. The sacrament is not a reward for good behavior in the past but a model for what it means to live rightly in the present and future.

Because of a centuries-old misreading of Paul, Christians have engaged in untold agony by examining themselves in advance of a eucharistic celebration and asking, "Am I worthy to receive communion this week?" Usually the answer has been "No!" And logically so. Who is worthy of God's grace? More to the point, who needs grace if worthiness exists? By definition, grace is only for the unworthy.

The examination to which Paul exhorts us is of a different sort and after the fact: "What have we, the church, learned as a result of seeing God's way proclaimed at the eucharistic feast? How do we view differently the rest of creation, because in the bread and wine we have found the creator's universal love set forth? How have we used for the service of others the strength offered us there?" A careful reading of 1 Corinthians 11:27-29 suggests that Paul is speaking of just such a corporate post-communion self-examination, not an earlier introspection that drives individuals away from the table of the Lord. We are responsible for the use of what we have received. But if we have received nothing because we deemed ourselves unworthy, what then? How superb an irony, that a commendable sense of unworthiness actually should become a loophole for lack of responsiveness to the gospel. Likely that is a real spiritual danger, one that flies in the face of covenant faithfulness to the God who above all else is gracious to us—and yearns deeply to make us gracious to one another and to the whole created order.

## THE SUPPERS IN THE SYNOPTICS

Each writing to a separate community of early Christians, Matthew, Mark, and Luke provide accounts of Jesus' supper in the upper room on the evening of his arrest. Despite differences in detail, these three accounts are remarkably similar and clearly relate to the church practice described by Paul in 1 Corinthians. To try to pull the four accounts into absolute harmony of detail is to miss the point. What is crucial is that every Christian community in the New Testament seems to have practiced and found deep meaning in a meal centered on Jesus' habit of eating and drinking with his followers.

*Habit* is here a crucial term, for the accounts of the upper room meal must be read in the context of all the rest of Jesus' feasting and of his use of stories about eating and drinking in his parables; we have set forth much of that in chapter 1. Such eating and drinking is characteristic of Jesus' ministry and is not some idiosyncratic event added at the end. Still, the cross gives new meaning to all that has preceded it, and so the church quickly found in its communal meal that which is intimately attached to the suffering and death of the Savior.

Persistent tradition has given the name "institution narrative" to the story of the supper in the upper room as found in Matthew 26:26-29, Mark 14:22-25, and Luke 22:15-20. The term is useful in giving a specific identifying title to a crucial biblical account. But it is misleading unless understood in a qualified and limited way. In his magisterial work *The Shape of the Liturgy*, Gregory Dix noted half a century ago that Jesus did not actually institute something in the sense of starting from scratch.[5] What Jesus did by his death and resurrection was to give far deeper meaning both to this final meal and his earlier meals, so that the church's meal could be seen as nothing other than a Christian Passover feast—a celebration of escape from servitude and death. In the

Exodus, the Hebrews were released from slavery to Pharaoh and from death in the sea and wilderness; this they remembered (in the sense of *anamnesis*) in the Passover feast. In Jesus' death and resurrection, creation was released from bondage to sin and from decay and death in the judgment; this the church remembers in the Eucharist.

As Passover commemorates the covenant between God and Israel, so also the Eucharist is the sign of the covenant Christ has opened to all by the sacrifice on the cross. Thus the cup of the Eucharist is the blood that seals the new covenant, even as the blood of the paschal lamb sealed the old covenant and ensured protection from the doomful angel of death, who passed over the homes of those with painted doorposts; and the bread of the Eucharist is the eternal Lamb of God on which the people feast (Exodus 12).[6]

What is of greater interest for us in the Synoptic Gospels than the "institution" narrative is a separate account given by Luke in his Emmaus story (Luke 24:13-35). Following the resurrection, Jesus appears to two of his followers, though they do not recognize him. As the day is over when they reach their home, Cleopas and his unnamed companion (his wife?) invite Jesus to spend the evening with them. "When he was at the table with them" the incognito risen One "took bread, blessed and broke it, and gave it to them." After he vanished from their sight, the two testified to disciples huddled in Jerusalem that "he had been made known to them in the breaking of the bread."

This story is crucial for the contemporary church because it stands in judgment over our preoccupation with the upper room on Thursday evening as the dominant focus of our Eucharists. Luke reports of Jesus in the upper room that he "took a loaf of bread, and when he had given thanks, he broke it and gave it to them" (22:19) and two chapters later tells of the risen One who "took bread, blessed and broke it, and gave it to them." Luke was too careful a writer for this similarity of language to be mistaken for an accident. Instead it is a powerful theological affirmation: The pre- and post-resurrection meals cannot be separated. If the Thursday meal was to be seen as a Passover feast, the joyful theme of God's deliverance therein is heightened by the Sunday meal. But even if the Thursday meal is to be seen as one of gloom and foreboding in the face of death, the Sunday meal announces the victory of the resurrection, thus transforming what went before.

What cannot be accepted as Luke's meaning is that the Thursday meal is to be seen as powerfully somber, and that the church is to continue this mood in all its Eucharists, while ignoring the joyful meal at Emmaus. And yet this is what the church has largely done for many centuries; the Supper of the Lord has been a kind of perpetual Holy Thursday evening inserted awkwardly and infrequently into the Sunday morning schedule.

I recall, early in my ministry, hearing my Methodist bishop exhort all of his clergy, saying: "Whenever you observe Holy Communion, you must sing one of two hymns—either 'When I Survey the Wondrous Cross' or 'In the Cross of Christ I Glory.' " In other words, he meant that the sacrament is always a reminder of Holy Thursday evening and Good Friday. More recently a United Methodist bishop publicly stated that the sacrament is inappropriate for Christmas Eve, for we should not mar the happy event of Jesus' birth with a solemn reminder of his death. That sentiment is reflected by all those people who shake their heads at the suggestion that the principal service on Easter Day should be eucharistic. "But," they object, well-schooled in the somberness of the sacrament, "how can you do something so sad on a day that is supposed to be so happy?" Obviously, the Emmaus meal theology has been stricken from popular Christian consciousness as if it had never been written.

We do well to be wary of a chirpy over-reaction that fastens onto the joy of resurrection and fails to see that no one can rise from the dead except by first dying. Nothing is gained if we replace one distortion with another. So we do well to follow carefully the lead of the Synoptic Gospels as they join death and resurrection in an indissoluble bond. Anything less is either too good to be true or too desolate to be endured in the name of the Gospel.

## THE EUCHARIST IN THE FOURTH GOSPEL

Because Jesus' baptism is given short shrift in John's Gospel and the meal in the upper room is absent altogether, until recently it was asserted that of the Gospels, the Fourth was the least sacramental in outlook. Now it is increasingly asserted that John's Gospel is the most sacramental of the four. Instead of packaging its sacramental teaching in discrete events in the ministry of Jesus, that teaching pervades the entire book in subtle but insistent ways. Thus eucharistic meanings are seen in the turning of water into wine at Cana (not reported in the Synoptics) and in the feeding of the thousands. More particularly, Jesus' breakfast with the disciples on the lakeshore (while an addition to the original book) is seen as a kind of parallel to Luke's Emmaus meal; the risen One is known in the familiar act of eating with the disciples (John 21:9-14).

Of greatest importance, however, is the long discussion on the bread of life in John 6. The discourse grows out of the feeding of the five thousand and the subsequent return of many the next day. Jesus deflects their desire for another free meal by contrasting earthly food with "the bread from heaven." The whole discussion could be seen as at best tangential to the Eucharist, were it not for the turn the passage takes in verses 51-56. Until then Jesus has been discussing only bread in its literal and metaphorical senses. Suddenly he connects the heavenly bread with his own flesh given for the life of the world (v. 51), and then explicitly introduces the drinking of his blood as well as the eating of his flesh in this assertion: "Those who eat my flesh and drink my blood have eternal life, and I will raise them up on the last day; for my flesh is true food and my blood is true drink. Those who eat my flesh and drink my blood abide in me, and I in them" (vv. 54-56).

Only the strangest kind of thinking can argue that all this has nothing to do with eucharistic eating and drinking in the community of faith. Certainly the passage should not be construed to approve some mechanistic view of salvation. It is not the eating and drinking as such that give life. It is Christ who gives life, but the life-giving Christ is not some ethereal entity disconnected from human existence. The life-giving Christ is the same Word made flesh for us (John 1:1-18). God's incarnational action in Christ is presented in the Eucharist again and again for the life of the world. This we grasp only by faith. The manifestations of God in the earthly manner of the Eucharist elicit faith and enable it to flourish.

## FEASTING IN HEAVEN

Feasting with Christ on earth is done, as we have seen, in anticipation of feasting with Christ in heaven. Early in the book of the Revelation to John, Jesus addresses the church in Laodicea, saying, "Listen! I am standing at the door, knocking; if you hear my voice and open the door, I will come in to you and eat with you, and you with me" (3:20).

The vision is consonant with the reference in Jesus' teaching of the great wedding feast of heaven (Matthew 22:1-14). A monarch plans a grand banquet, to which many are invited. When the selected guests decline to attend, the invitation is extended widely until the wedding hall is filled. What is crucial is that this final invitation is exceedingly gracious. Those sent out to find guests gathered "all whom they found, both good and bad."

Luke includes a very similar story, although the banquet is not a wedding feast (Luke 14:16-24). The host sends a servant out, instructing, "Go out at once into the streets and lanes of the town and bring in the poor, the crippled, the blind, and the lame" (v. 21). When there is still room in the banquet hall, again the host instructs the servant, "Go out into the roads and lanes, and compel people to come in, so that my house may be filled."

In both stories, this divine desire to fill the house evokes judgment against those who reject the invitation. This same confluence of grace and judgment characterizes the brief account of the heavenly supper in Revelation 19. First there is the declaration, "Blessed are those who are invited to the marriage supper of the Lamb" (v. 9). Then the wrath of God goes forth against evil. Finally, great birds in heaven are summoned: "Come, gather for the great supper of God, to eat the flesh of kings, the flesh of captains, the flesh of the mighty, the flesh of horses and their riders—flesh of all, both free and slave, both small and great" (vv. 17-18). The carnage of the scavenger birds is described, but not the great supper for the saints, which presumably follows.

Strange and ugly though all these words of judgment may sound, they have a purpose: God's final feast will be a banquet of purity. All that is evil, all that resists God will be not merely excluded but abolished. Those who eat the supper need fear no evil, for this is not a table in the midst of the enemies (as in Psalm 23) but in the utter absence of the enemies. The great banquet will celebrate God's final victory over unrighteousness. It will indeed be redemptive.

The final eating described in heaven pertains to twelve kinds of fruit, one for each month (22:2); the leaves of the tree are for the healing of "the nations"—that is, the Gentiles. Wait a minute! What are Gentiles doing in the city of heaven? Weren't the Gentiles and their monarchs slain in 19:15-21? Yet they turn up again in 21:24: "The nations [the Gentiles] will walk by [God's] light, and the kings of the earth will bring their glory into it." Is it perhaps that all of this confusing—sometimes seemingly irrational—data points to God's mysterious redemption? In ways beyond our understanding, that divine graciousness draws into the eternal banquet hall those who have been despised and cast out.[7] All may come. Including us!

# CHAPTER THREE

# FAITH SEEKING UNDERSTANDING

Theology is sometimes defined as "faith seeking understanding." Through our encounter with God we come to a conviction or trust; then we feel the need to give some reasonable account of that deeply held belief. To put it another way, after we experience, we try to explain. It is a natural process for human beings. But in the deepest experiences of faith, explanation will never be complete, and therefore can never be final. Theology is faith seeking understanding, not faith seizing understanding, let alone faith explaining everything to the last detail.

The church first came to know the risen Lord in the breaking of the bread, and then began to ask the question, "But how can this be, that Christ is made known to us in our service of praise and thanksgiving?" A great variety of answers followed. To trace the full intellectual history of eucharistic doctrine would require volumes of technical and often tedious data. At the risk of great oversimplification, we can here examine only briefly the major streams of thinking that fed into and flowed out of the Catholic-Protestant controversies about the Eucharist in the Reformation era. These debates still influence our understanding, often in ways we do not even recognize.

As Christianity moved out of the Hebraic world, with its concept of *anamnesis,* into the world of more abstract Western thinking, the church began to interact with the major schools of Greek philosophy: those of Plato and of his disciple, Aristotle. For a millennium these systems dominated Christian thought. But just prior to the Reformation they were challenged by new patterns of thinking. At the time of the great religious conflict in the sixteenth century, in its official teaching the Roman Catholic Church held tenaciously to the old systems; to varying degrees Luther, Zwingli, and Calvin moved in new directions, and diverged from one another as they did so. Subsequent Catholicism and Protestantism tended to perpetuate the sixteenth-century differences, carrying them into our own time.

Now, as the Eucharist once again has become more important to all of us, both Protestants and Catholics are raising fundamental questions about the meaning of the experience of knowing our risen Lord in the breaking of the bread. There is a reasonable possibility that we can escape from the sixteenth-century gridlock and come to a satisfying ecumenical solution—not a single, uniform doctrine, but a dialogue that makes possible a sharing of the sacrament in the setting of mutual respect and affection. But we will not get out of the tangle of half a millennium until we understand the forces that have alienated us in the past, and that threaten to paralyze efforts to bring about reconciliation among the churches in our day. Therefore we turn now to an examination of these forces in broad outline.

## EUCHARISTIC PRESENCE AS EXPLAINED BY PLATONISM

In the Hellenistic world, the church encountered the philosophical system of Plato (c. 427–347 B.C.), adapted by the Christian thinker Plotinus (A.D. 205–270). This adaptation, known as Neo-Platonism, gained wide currency in the Western church through the influence of the fourth-century African theologian, Augustine of Hippo. Within this Platonic mode of thinking, the church arrived at a cogent way of "solving" (or at least domesticating) the mystery as to how bread and wine can be the body and blood of Christ.

Central to the Platonic system was the question, What gives things their identity? Why, it was asked, is a tree a tree? And how is it that the various tall, woody-stemmed plants we call trees have such differing characteristics? Some bear lovely flowers; others do not. Some produce fruit and others nuts and still others nothing at all that we consider edible; indeed some produce toxic substances. Some have narrow needles that stay green in all climates; others have broad leaves that in the less temperate climates are shed in the autumn and grow anew in the spring. So what makes all of these things fit into the single category "tree"?

In answer, Platonists suggested that there is something shared by all trees that exists apart from any particular tree. Since all trees partake of it, that prior something is a "universal," and the trees we see are its "particulars." In our contemporary way of speaking, we might be inclined to call this universal a "Super Tree." (Platonists preferred a term usually translated as "form," "idea," or "ideal.")

Super Tree cannot be seen by us; it exists before and beyond our physical world, and thereby gives a common identity to the objects we call trees, be they peach, walnut, pine, or hemlock. Each individual tree on earth is a kind of incomplete grasping after, an imperfect, shadowy manifestation of, Super Tree.

Each particular tree that we see around us is a "thing" (Latin, *res*) dependent upon the prior universal (Super Tree). Since the universal exists "before the thing" (Latin, *ante rem*), the technical name for all of this is "Extreme Realism." The term does not mean, as we might think, that something is very, very, very real. It means that the true and most basic identity of the thing (Super Tree) exists before any particular thing (peach, walnut, pine, or hemlock) can come into existence. Christian Platonists, who clearly believed in a Creator behind all we see, readily located the universal forms or patterns in heaven, even in the mind of the God by whom all earthly things are made.[1]

If this kind of thinking seems totally alien to us, and particularly if we suspect it of being contrary to biblical thought, it should be noted that something at least closely akin is already present in the late New Testament period. In the book of Hebrews, Christ is seen as the true priest who ministers in the heavenly sanctuary, that "true tent that the Lord, and not any mortal, has set up" (8:2). When human priests minister in earthly tents, these are but sketches, shadows, or copies of what is in heaven (8:5; 9:23-24). Even the law given us directly by God is seen by the writer of Hebrews to be "only a shadow of the good things to come and not the true form of these realities" (10:1). If this is not Plato's "extreme realism" in the midst of the New Testament, it is difficult to know what keeps it from being that.

Because we have grown up in what we might call "the modern, scientific era" (more correctly, the era of empiricism), this point of view is so odd we are inclined to scoff at it. An object, we believe, is what we discover it to be by careful investigation; we cannot regard it as a mere shadow or sketch only approximating and depending upon some deeper identity that exists in another, prior world. For example, how many architects, when designing homes, think of themselves as trying to approximate True House out there somewhere through styles as diverse as Cape Cod, Neo-Georgian, Bauhaus, and Post-Modern? This simply is not our way of thinking. But it was a sincerely and firmly held belief in ancient times that the true identity of things exists apart from the physical manifestations we experience. And in the framework of that understanding, the church provided the following way of talking about bread and wine as being the body and blood of Christ.

On earth we have various kinds of bread (whole wheat, rye, white, sourdough) and of wine (burgundy, chablis, chianti, port). All of these are shadows of The Bread and The Wine that existed in the mind of God before any earthly loaves could be baked or grapes fermented. But along with the heavenly forms that give identity to earthly food and drink, there is in heaven the risen Christ. Does not scripture refer to Christ as the True Bread from heaven (John 6:25-59, esp. v. 32) and the True Vine sent from God (John 15:1-11, esp. v. 1)?

So then, what occurs in the Eucharist can be explained as a change in the basic identity of the bread and wine on the eucharistic table. We come to church bearing bread from our ovens and wine from our vineyards. They are bread and wine because they are shadows or sketches of The Bread and The Wine in heaven, which call into being all loaves of bread and all jugs of wine in the world. The bread and wine we bring to church are the "particulars" of The Bread and The Wine just as oaks and pines are particulars of The Tree in the mind of God (Plato's Super Tree).

In the course of the liturgy, however, a transfer of identity occurs. As a result, the earthly bread is made real not by The Bread in heaven which shapes all ordinary loaves, but by the True Bread of Heaven, Jesus Christ, risen and enthroned. Similarly, the wine we bring ceases to be related to The Wine in heaven that identifies all ordinary vintages and instead takes a new and deeper identifying meaning from the True Vine, Jesus Christ. In this sense, through the agency of the prayers of the church and the mysterious work of God, the eucharistic bread and wine truly are the body and blood of Christ according to Platonic definitions.

But note carefully that this has nothing whatever to do with the chemical composition of the bread and wine; they still look, taste, smell, and feel exactly as they did when they left the oven and the wine cellar. Nothing physical or observable occurs. What is changed is the external identity of the thing, not identifiable characteristics of the thing. In other words, nothing is altered that can be tested by scientific methods, for the whole system of prior universals that give meaning to particulars lies outside the domain of scientific investigation. The fact that the sacred bread and wine on the altar do not resemble the physical flesh and blood of Jesus is of no more concern than that a pine tree does not greatly resemble a peach tree and that both are different from Super Tree.

No matter how arcane or ridiculous all of this seems to us, for a Platonically oriented culture the church thus achieved a satisfying explanation as to how bread and wine can "be" the body and blood of the Lord. With the explanation came a difficulty, however.

To focus on a change of identity that occurs within an act of worship invites the question, And precisely when and how does the change occur? Liturgical remembrance in its Hebraic sense (*anamnesis*) is a unified dynamic process. There is little temptation to pinpoint within the process a specific moment that is more crucial than any other, let alone to explain exactly what occurs in that identifiable moment. But move from that to the occurrence of a transforming event, and sooner or later theologians will feel compelled to debate (and even to decide) when and how the change of identity occurs. Does the transformation occur when the priest says, "This is my Body" (the words of institution) or when the priest prays for the power of the Holy Spirit (the *Epiclesis*)? Does the change occur by virtue of the correct words being uttered by the priest, or by some other means? If the former, what happens if the priest accidentally skips a key phrase or says the wrong word?

Such a desire to isolate the time and manner of the transformation results in a legalistic preoccupation that can erode liturgical piety and distort the church's prayerful action into a source of superstition. We will see the consequences when in chapter 4 we look at the medieval emphasis on arriving at the church "in time to see the miracle happen."

## EUCHARISTIC PRESENCE AS EXPLAINED BY ARISTOTELIANISM

Throughout the centuries, Platonists and Aristotelians vied for popularity and power in philosophical circles. Aristotle had modified Plato's explanation for how things come to have a specific identity, and the church had to relate this also to its experience of knowing the risen Lord in the breaking of the bread.

For Aristotle, universal identity did not exist prior to a particular thing but along with the thing itself, indeed "in the thing" itself. Hence this position is known by the Latin phrase *in re* and is called "Moderate Realism." It is "moderate" in the sense that the particular thing is less separated from its true identity than is the case in the "Extreme Realism" of the Platonists. Nevertheless, for Aristotelians, core identity was still independent of the physical characteristics of the thing.

Theologians who followed Aristotle taught that all physical objects have two components. One is substance, the core identifying quality, which can no more be observed scientifically than can the heavenly forms of the Platonists. It simply has to be taken on faith, for example, that all trees have within them the characteristics of "treeness"; that is what identifies them as trees rather than as rocks or clouds.

Alongside the identifying substance shared by all things that bear the same name ("tree," in our example), there is a second, less enduring set of characteristics that vary from one particular to another. Thus all trees share the substance we can call "treeness," but various trees are distinctive because of other, variable characteristics, including size, shape, hardness of wood, type of seeds, kind of foliage, longevity, and the like. These observable differences have little to do with the core identity ("treeness") and are called "accidents" in contrast to "substance." If the term seems odd, it is akin to our saying that the color of a person's eyes, hair, and skin are "accidents of birth" that do not make one human or prevent one from being human.

To put it another way, the accidents are all of those things that can be described, measured, or tested. They exist alongside the crucial identifying "substance" that no scientific investigation can locate or examine. Followers of Aristotle simply took it for granted that a tree cannot be a tree unless there is something that makes it a tree other than its observable characteristics.

The crucial difference between the two ancient philosophical systems is that Christian Platonists believed the true identity of a thing to be in a perfect form or divine pattern in the mind of God prior to the creation of the object. Christian Aristotelians located the true identity within the object itself—in the "substance" of that object, put there by God as a part of the creative act.

Within the Aristotelian framework the church also had to make a defensible case for believing bread and wine could "be" the body and blood of Jesus Christ. Given the assumptions, we can readily see that whole wheat, rye, white, and sourdough loaves all were seen as bread because they share the common substance "bread," which exists independently of the different kinds of dough and is within each loaf.

Now the explanation of the words "This is my body" can be readily guessed: At the Eucharist the substance within the loaf changes. Whereas the loaf as baked in the oven at home and brought to church had within it the substance "bread," in the course of the liturgy it comes to have within the substance "Body of Christ." So also with the wine, which comes to have in it the substance "Blood of Christ." Because at the Lord's Table there occurs a transfer or transformation of substance, this way of understanding the Eucharist is called "transubstantiation."

As it was in Plato's system, so also it was in Aristotle's. There is no way a scientist can prove or disprove that any change has occurred. Often Protestants have poked fun at the classical Roman Catholic doctrine of transubstantiation by saying, "But after the consecration in the Mass, the bread doesn't look, taste, or feel any different; certainly it doesn't resemble the human flesh of Jesus in any observable way." But those who reject transubstantiation on such grounds simply do not understand the basic assumptions that everything has an identifying inner substance and that this substance is independent of all observable characteristics.

The real difficulty with transubstantiation is that most of us—Protestant or Roman Catholic—no longer are able to accept such assumptions, or even to understand them in full form. The descriptions given here are immensely simplified, in the hope that the basic notion can be grasped by those who do not wish to study the complexities of ancient and medieval philosophy. But knowing the complexities makes it harder—not easier—for twentieth century people to grant the assumptions. What is important to understand is that in earlier times those assumptions were not only acceptable but were quite comfortable to the intellectuals of the day. Indeed, those assumptions were a part of the accepted science of that era. And the church, far from dismissing science as irrelevant to theology, provided a means by which one could readily move between fact (as delineated by science) and faith (as experienced and transmitted by the church).

The Platonic explanation for the presence of Christ in the Eucharist introduced the questions of time and manner: When during the worship service does the change occur? By what means does it happen to occur? The Aristotelian explanation complicated things by adding to that a preoccupation with the question of space. If a transfer of Platonic identity occurs in heaven, where Christ sits in glory (as for the Extreme Realists), that is one thing. But if the transfer of substance occurs within the bread itself on the altar, that is something else, for then we must ask where the original substance goes. Is the substance of the heavenly body of the risen Lord altered or diminished because it has entered into the bread and wine in a church building on earth (indeed in thousands of church buildings day in and day out)?

To deal with such problems of space, theologians came up with three possibilities:

1. The most troubling option assumes that substance, while not scientifically observable, nevertheless takes up a fixed and limited amount of space. Therefore, the original substances of bread and wine either must be destroyed or must vacate the accidents of bread and wine in order to make room for the new substances. Hence this is called the "annihilation" or "evacuation" theory. It raises a crucial problem concerning the risen and ascended Lord. If the substance of Christ's heavenly body comes down to earth to fill a fixed amount of space, is not the substance in heaven diminished as a result? How often can this occur before the heavenly substance is depleted in such a way that the substance of Christ's risen body finally ceases to exist in heaven (and consequently can no longer produce transubstantiation on earth)?

2. A preferable option in effect allows space within the accidents for a new substance to be added. Thus the original substances of bread and wine are retained, and the substances of the body and blood of Christ enter and exist alongside them. This can technically be called "consubstantiation"—*con* being a Latin prefix meaning "with." Thus the new substance coexists with the old. But that still leaves the question as to whether the heavenly substances of Christ's body and blood are not diminished as these are transferred to earthly bread and wine. Furthermore, since substance establishes identity in the Aristotelian system, it must be asked: Can a thing have two separate core identities at once?

3. The most alluring (and the most elusive) option is that the transformation of the bread and wine does not affect Christ in heaven at all because it occurs by multiplication, not relocation. The substances bread and wine do not evacuate the accidents, nor do they reside there along with something new; they are themselves totally changed into the same thing that exists in heaven, without in any way depleting those heavenly substances.

This is transubstantiation as it was ultimately defined by the Roman Catholic Church.[2]

Once again we must say that no matter how puzzling, trivial, or even amusing all of this may be to us, it was of cardinal importance in earlier centuries. Had the church not sought to understand its faith in terms of the intellectual concepts of its day, it would have sacrificed integrity. And no matter how alien the ancient systems seem to our kind of "scientific" thinking, they were in fact the accepted scientific systems of earlier eras. Not to attempt to reconcile the eucharistic Presence of Christ with both Extreme and Moderate Realism would have opened the church to the charge of retreating into magic, superstition, or plain simple-mindedness.

Yet in addressing these philosophical systems, the church invited unfortunate consequences. Among these were preoccupations with time (When precisely in the liturgy does the moment of transformation occur?), space (How do you make room for the new substance in the bread and wine, and how does this affect Christ's risen body in heaven, if at all?), and manner (What words and ritual acts must be used if the necessary change is to take place?). These regrettable consequences were already on the doorstep of the church when the movement we call the Protestant Reformation approached.

## THE NOMINALIST CHALLENGE TO THE STATUS QUO

In the fourteenth and fifteenth centuries, both Plato and Aristotle were dealt mortal blows by a new viewpoint that said, in effect, "A plague on both your houses. Trees aren't called trees because of any universal (Super Tree) that exists before any particular tree can come into being, nor because at creation God imbeds in them an identifying inner substance (Treeness). They are called trees because human beings have named them that, based on an organizational scheme humanly devised."

That is, first there exist the things we experience. As humans, we insist on making order out of everything around us; so we put into categories those things that have certain resemblances (as defined by us): trees, both hardwood and softwood; rocks, both igneous and sedimentary; clouds, both cumulus and cirrus. Human beings organize things into categories and then assign a name to each grouping.

The key word is *name,* in Latin, *nomen.* Hence this position is called "Nominalism." Names, this philosophical system assumes, do not exist before there is something to which to attach them. Has anyone ever wasted time producing a list of previously unused words from which names must be selected for new inventions? Of course not! First we invent something, and then we find a name to describe it appropriately. Names come after the thing; hence the Latin phrase for this position is *post rem.* Identity exists not ahead of the thing (Extreme Realism's *ante rem*), nor within it (Moderate Realism's *in re*), but after the thing (Nominalism's *post rem*).

The writer of Genesis 2:19 was a proto-nominalist. Whatever Adam called every living creature, that was its name. So also was Shakespeare's Romeo when he assured Juliet that "a rose by any other name would smell as sweet." Almost all of us today, whether we realize it or not, are Nominalists. We take it for granted that the term *tree* is a matter of convenience, not of an absolute God-given identity.

It would have been quite possible to separate hardwoods and softwoods into two distinct categories that could have been designated "loompahs" and "beborts," respectively. Then there would have been no "trees" at all! We take it for granted that a tree is a tree simply because we have agreed to name it that in our attempt to organize reality in some logical way. But logic admits of more than one organizational possibility. And different language systems use quite different names for their categories, even when agreeing with each other about the basic organizational schemes.

The Nominalist viewpoint, so congenial to our tastes, emerged prior to the Reformation and has since become the prevailing assumption. At first theologians did not try to adjust the standard eucharistic explanations to fit in with Nominalism, perhaps for fear of being charged with heresy. But the break with medieval Catholicism gave the Protestant reformers the latitude to adjust their eucharistic thinking to fit Nominalist assumptions, as they did, though in divergent ways.

Because they were reacting strongly against the abuses related to the timing and manner of "the miracle" in the Mass, the Reformers largely avoided any concern about "when" in the liturgy the crucial moment could occur, and similarly played down precision about words and gestures necessary to effect the eucharistic Presence. But even as they challenged the earlier schools of thought, the Reformers could not free themselves from the category of space that had preoccupied the old thinking: If the Body of Christ is present on the altar, how does this affect Christ's body in heaven? Granted, for Nominalists there was no longer any substance to take up space in bread and wine; still, how can Christ be in heaven and also on the table in church, let alone on thousands of such tables simultaneously?

Because the principal Reformers dealt differently with the issue, we now look at Luther, Zwingli, and Calvin separately.

## LUTHER: UBIQUITOUS PRESENCE

Luther sought to solve the puzzle of space with his doctrine of the "ubiquity" of Christ's risen body. Ordinarily, he granted, physical bodies can occupy only one finite space at a time; but the body of the Lord, while ordinary in its humanity in the incarnation, is transformed by virtue of the resurrection. This conviction allowed Luther to speculate that Christ's risen body could transcend certain limitations common to ordinary objects.

Luther also drew heavily on the ancient church's teaching about the nature of Christ. With great conflict and precision, the church in the fourth and fifth centuries had formulated a doctrine of the incarnation that included what is called a "hypostatic union": In the one person of Christ are found both human nature and divine nature. These are neither collapsed into one (as the Monophysite party taught) nor do they stand separately side by side (as the Nestorian party contended). Rather, two intact natures interpenetrate each other in the one person of Christ. In the Eastern Orthodox churches this interpenetration is known as *perichoresis,* and in the West is referred to as *communicatio idiomatum.*

Luther believed this "communication of the idioms" in the nature of Christ provided a way out of the muddle about the spatial aspects of the eucharistic Presence. The omnipresence of the divine nature so interpenetrates the incarnate human nature that Christ's risen body is capable of being everywhere at once. Hence Luther taught that Christ's Presence is "ubiquitous" (from the Latin *ubique,* meaning "everywhere").

This understanding provided Luther with a very rich doctrine of the revelatory power of Christ in the created world. So also it prevented his eucharistic doctrine from being narrow, since Christ's presence in the Supper is not some unique and detached epiphany, disjointed from the rest of life; instead it is the clue as to what all of life is really about.

Luther elaborated his understanding as follows: The risen Christ fills all creation around us and holds all things in creation together (see Colossians 1:15-17). But our eyes are clouded over by sin, and we fail to recognize Christ in our midst. We come to church wearing, as it were, a heavy veil over our faces, through which we can see Christ's presence in our world dimly, if at all. In our eucharistic experience, that veil is momentarily lifted. In bread and wine we discover the presence of Christ that we ought to see every day in everything good around us. Because of this gift of sacramental clarity, we leave the church with new insight, but the cares and temptations of the world assault us. Again the veil descends, so that we no longer see the way in which the risen One fills the whole creation. Thus we must come back to the Table of the Lord repeatedly to have our vision cleared.

There is great merit in that understanding of Christ's interaction with the world around us. The difficulty is that Luther could not quite get free of having to think of both the Lord's risen body and the eucharistic Presence as taking up space. The "where" question plagued him.

Ultimately Lutheranism answered that question with a theological formulation: The body of Christ is given to believers "in, with, and under" the physical bread of the Lord's Table. Here was an attempt to remain faithful to the sacramental heritage of the church while rejecting transubstantiation as an adequate explanation. But note the way in which "in," "with," and "under" all continue to imply a spatial dimension to the Presence in relation to the physical bread; Lutheranism had not completely shaken itself free from the Moderate Realism of the Aristotelians.[3]

## ZWINGLI: MEMORIALISM

Ulrich (Huldreich) Zwingli, a former Roman Catholic priest who headed the Reformation movement in Zurich, was familiar with the views of Luther, his counterpart in Saxony. But to Zwingli, the Lutheran theory of ubiquity was as incomprehensible as transubstantiation. Scripture and the creeds affirmed that Christ sits in heaven, at the right hand of the Father; nothing more could be said—or should be imagined.

Therefore Zwingli taught that Christ spiritually is in the hearts of believers who, according to Paul, constitute Christ's spiritual "body" on earth; but the Lord's physical body is in heaven and nowhere else. Bread and wine are visual reminders of the Savior's sacred passion and death, which communicants rightly contemplate at the Lord's Table. Those who come with deep faith may indeed be edified, and those who come with a sagging faith may have it bolstered; but in both cases the benefit occurs because of the faith the believers bring to the experience, not because the experience engenders faith within them.

Zwingli's views led him to make very explicit what had always been implicit in earlier discussions of the meaning of the sacrament: the function of the word *is* in the formulae "This is my body" and "This is my blood." In contrast to the general assumption that *is* implies an identification of being, Zwingli insisted that *is* means "symbolizes" in a commemorative sense: "This bread and wine remind you of my body and blood offered upon the cross."

For Zwingli, it is the task of the communicant to meditate in faith on the passion as historic event. The eucharistic elements point to this event, but the elements do not uniquely present that passion, nor do they convey to us its benefits except as all faithful contemplation of the cross may do so. The function of the elements is to focus such contemplation, to call to clearer remembrance the historic events of our salvation.

The strength or weakness of the Zwinglian position depends on how vibrant an understanding of *symbol* is implied. If the symbol is seen to participate deeply and richly in the thing symbolized, well and good. But if regarded as "only" a symbol, or as a "mere symbol," the implied weakening leaves the Eucharist as a kind of vague aid to devotion, likely more dependent upon the subjective mood of the believer than on any objective reality communicated to the believer.

Zwingli's position often is called "memorialism," but its understanding of remembrance is conceptual and cerebral. Thus it is quite different from the Hebraic understanding of *anamnesis,* which had largely slipped from the consciousness of the church.[4] In Hebrew piety, memory was an active reliving of the past by doing now ritually what then had been done actually. In Zwinglian piety, memory is the thoughtful but rather passive contemplation of events that are long past.

## CALVIN: VIRTUALISM

John Calvin (1509–64) saw both merit and danger in the positions of those who preceded him by a generation—Luther (1483–1546) and Zwingli (1484–1531). Like Luther, Calvin wanted to affirm the sacramental tradition of the Supper of the Lord as a divine gift that engenders faith in us because it proclaims the gospel to us with power more clearly than words alone can do. A bare memorialism of the Zwinglian kind could not satisfy. But Luther's doctrine of ubiquity had no appeal for Calvin; with Zwingli, the French reformer believed the body of the risen Lord to exist in heaven and there alone.

Yet Calvin saw a middle way. By the power of the Holy Spirit, we are mysteriously joined with the risen Lord in the Supper. The Spirit is able to overcome the barrier of distance, so that the body of Christ on earth (the church) is united with the risen

Lord's heavenly body in the liturgy of bread and wine. The eucharistic elements are not transmuted into something else, nor are they merely visual aids to the faith we bring to the holy table. The bread and wine convey the power of Christ through the wonderful action of the Spirit. This is a matter less to be explained than enjoyed.

Still, even when protesting that no satisfactory explanation of the Presence of Christ is to be sought, let alone achieved, Calvin cannot escape the urge to deal with the problem of space. If for the Aristotelians the body of the risen Lord comes down upon the altar, for Calvin the body of believers momentarily (if mysteriously) is transported to heaven. Calvin joins the opening words of the Latin eucharistic prayer, *Sursum Corda* ("Lift up your hearts"), with an admonition in Colossians 3:1: "Seek the things that are above, where Christ is, seated at the right hand of God." Thus Calvin's liturgy of the Supper includes this exhortation: "Let us raise our hearts and minds on high, where Jesus Christ is in the glory of his Father."[5]

This raising up can be achieved only by the power of the Holy Spirit, thus giving Calvin's teaching a commendably strong emphasis on the role of the Spirit in the Eucharist. This corrected a weakness in Western liturgies, from which a specific *epiklesis* (prayer for the ministry of the Spirit) had disappeared (though it had remained as a central feature of Eastern Orthodox liturgies).

Because of this stress on the power of the Spirit and also the powerful nature of the grace of Christ in the sacrament, Calvin's position is known as "virtualism" from the Latin word for power, *virtus*. (Sometimes his point of view is called "dynamic virtualism," though this is a tautology since *dynamis* is the Greek term for "power.")

Now we must consider how these three Reformers interacted in ways that reverberate to the present.

## REFORMATION INTERACTION AND CONTINUING ISSUES

Luther and Zwingli, familiar with each other's eucharistic teaching, could come to no common understanding. Luther was determined to preserve the classical affirmation that the Eucharist is one means by which the risen Christ communicates with us—that is (to use traditional language), the sacrament is "a means of grace." He rejected misinterpretations that turned this into "conveyor-belt theology." Bread and wine do not automatically transmit saving grace to anyone who happens to come into contact with them, Luther insisted. Still, they are divinely chosen ways in which the truth of the gospel is proclaimed to the church. God acts through the Eucharist, revealing saving goodness to us. Again, using traditional terminology, Luther insisted that the Eucharist is an "effective sign"; it communicates what it signifies, making Christ's risen Presence effectively known in the church.

For Zwingli, this bordered too closely on medieval abuse, which seemed to turn the sacrament into magic and which quantified grace, so that the Mass achieved saving action, simply by being performed.[6] Luther, of course, knew this danger, but Zwingli reacted the more strongly by suggesting that the eucharistic action was directed from the church to God, not vice versa. Thus at the Lord's Supper believers affirm their faith by contemplating the central act of salvation. Insofar as the bread and wine are "signs" for Zwingli, they are but "bare signs" (Latin, *signa nuda*)—at best "props for faith" that reinforce but do not create awareness of Christ with us.

The dispute between Luther and Zwingli is something of a chicken-egg problem. Was their basic disagreement a philosophical dispute about the possibility of Christ's eucharistic Presence, which then led the one to affirm the sacrament as a means of grace while the other rejected this? Or was their basic disagreement a theological and practical one about the nature of grace and faith, so that Luther had to seek a philosophical explanation to buttress the concept of the sacrament as gracious sign, while Zwingli rejected such an explanation in order to maintain his bare memorialism? Or does the dispute have tangled roots in a soil even more complex due to factors of personal temperament, nationalistic tensions between Saxony and Switzerland, and issues of power in leading the reform movement?

We cannot know. Suffice it to say that having carried on extensive battles with pen and ink on a variety of issues, Luther and Zwingli agreed to meet face-to-face in the hope of coming to some resolution of their differences. This conference, held in the city of Marburg in 1529, is known as "The Marburg Colloquy." While they came to agreement on other matters, with respect to the nature of the Eucharist each left Marburg more entrenched in what he regarded as a position that could not admit to compromise.

In summary, the positions of these two Reformers can be encapsuled as follows. Luther said, "I believe the Lord is particularly made known in the breaking of the bread; since I cannot accept transubstantiation, I will explain the eucharistic Presence in another new way." Zwingli responded: "I cannot accept transubstantiation, nor can I explain eucharistic Presence in another new way that is satisfactory to me; therefore, I will not affirm that the Lord is particularly made known in the breaking of the bread." Between these positions stood Calvin, who took the first part of each statement: "I cannot accept transubstantiation, nor can I explain eucharistic Presence in any other way that is satisfactory to me; nevertheless I believe the Lord is particularly made known in the breaking of the bread."

For Calvin, such thinking was extremely uncharacteristic. He was trained as a lawyer, and his writing is tightly argued and often severely analytical. But when he comes to discuss the eucharistic Presence, he uses personal affirmation rather than impressive logical disputation. Indeed, he virtually breaks forth into song:

> Now if anyone asks me how this takes place, I shall not be ashamed to confess that it is a secret too lofty for either my mind to comprehend or my words to declare. And to speak more plainly, I rather experience than understand it.
>
> I rather exhort my readers . . . to attempt to rise much higher than I can guide them. For whenever this subject is considered, after I have done my utmost, I feel that I have spoken far beneath its dignity. And though the mind is more powerful in thought than the tongue in expression, it is too overcome and overwhelmed by the magnitude of the subject. All then that remains is to break forth in admiration of the mystery, which it is plain that the mind is inadequate to comprehend, or the tongue to express.[7]

Calvin did, of course, seek to understand the matter insofar as he could: The eucharistic Presence is the work of the Holy Spirit, who mysteriously unites us with Christ in the heavenly banquet. This is a far less comprehensive explanation than that of the medieval theologians or Luther, but it must be admitted that Calvin's intimation that we are united with Christ in the Supper because somehow the Spirit lifts us up to heaven (where Christ sits) is no less mystifying in the age of space travel than transubstantiation or ubiquitarianism.

It may be that had Calvin been at the Marburg Colloquy, he and Luther would have come to close agreement—but that Zwingli would still have gone away unconvinced. Certainly for Calvin, as for Luther, sacraments were effective signs and means of grace. Calvin would not identify the sign with the reality in any definable way; yet he insisted that the truth of the thing signified is certainly made present. This is a far cry from the usual interpretation of Zwingli's "bare signs" as visual aids useful for propping up a sagging faith. Zwingli's responsibility for the degree of bareness of his memorialism among his followers is another matter. Usually disciples outdo their teachers in zeal, and the instance of Zwingli's views may be no exception.

Suffice it to say that a gulf came to be fixed between Luther and Calvin, on the one side, and Zwingli and the Anabaptists on the other. Lutherans and Calvinists preserved the tradition of regarding the Eucharist as a sacrament—a means of grace offered to us by God, a form of proclaiming the gospel consisting of the word of promise ("Lo! I am with you always," for example) and signs (bread and wine) that seal the promise to us. Zwinglians and Anabaptists insisted instead that the Supper is only an ordinance—a kind of affirmation of faith that we offer to God as an indication of our obedience to Christ's order (hence the term *ordinance*), "Do this in remembrance of me." The crucial word in the last statement is *only*. Those on the sacramental side of the fence did not deny that Christ ordered the church to "Do this"; they simply asserted in addition that in the doing of it God offers us more than we ourselves can bring to the Supper. The sacrament is a divinely granted proclamation of the gospel, not simply a human affirmation of the gospel.

Furthermore, the sacramental side of the Reformation churches took very seriously the notion of the Eucharist as a "seal" that confirms a promise. Together the words related to God's promises (particularly expounded in preaching) and the seal of the sacrament authenticate the gospel to us. That is why Luther and Calvin wanted both sermon and Supper weekly, whereas Zwingli opted for weekly preaching but quarterly Eucharist.

The relation between words and seal can be set forth in contemporary experience as follows. Suppose you receive in the mail an ordinary looking envelope with "1600 Pennsylvania Avenue, Washington, D.C." typed on its upper left corner. Inside on equally plain, undecorated paper is the message: "The President of The United States invites you to a state dinner at the White House," followed by date, time, and details. Unless you are hopelessly naive, you will not appear at the executive mansion at the designated time; while the words are "right," there is nothing that visibly authenticates them. You realize that the president has not invited you to anything; instead someone has played a practical joke on you.

Suppose, on the other hand, that you receive a formal looking envelope, with your name written in calligraphy. Embossed in its corner are the words "The White House" and on its flap is the seal of the president in gold. There is an equally impressive inner envelope; within that is a formal invitation, again bearing the presidential seal. But beyond that the invitation is totally blank, apparently due to a misfeed at the engraver's. Now, though the invitation seems genuine, you cannot go to the White House because you have no idea to what you are being invited. Any genuine communication of this sort requires both words and authenticating signs.

That was the point of the sacramental side of the Reformation. The medieval Mass at which no sermon was preached was like the fancy invitation that bears no discernible message, and the Zwinglian preaching service from which the sacrament was absent was like a message deemed bogus in the absence of authenticating signs. God's promises come to us most amply only as words and signs are given together.

The eucharistic positions outlined above are the dominant and most influential, though by no means the only Reformation views. But other positions of the period (such as those of Martin Bucer or Johannes Oecolampadius) are variations on the three major themes, not distinctive constructions. Post-Reformation theologies among Protestants are primarily combinations and mutations of sixteenth-century formulations. But eventually, even among Lutherans and Calvinists, as among Anglicans (who were influenced by both), it was a form of Zwinglianism that won the day—despite the fact that the doctrinal statements of all these bodies insisted the Supper is a sacrament and not an ordinance only. This triumph of Zwinglianism had less to do with formal ecclesiastical decisions than with the reign of rationalism in Britain and across the European continent in the eighteenth century and with strains of pietism and revivalism that accentuated personal faith above the sacraments. Only of late has the dominance of a bare and reductionalistic memorialism been challenged.

The challenge has sometimes resulted in "neo" movements that seek to return to the teaching of the respective Reformers; at times these have bordered on a kind of liturgical fundamentalism more interested in restoring sixteenth-century doctrine and practice than in seeking to understand the faith in ways appropriate to our own time. This, in turn, has caused some Christians on the cutting edge of theology and social reform to disparage the sacrament as a vestige of the past or as the irrelevant hobby of a pious coterie. (It is said, for example, that the noted theologian William Inge, late dean of St. Paul's Cathedral, London, was once asked whether he studied liturgical theology. "No," he replied with great disdain, "nor do I collect postage stamps.")

From our contemporary standpoint, the major difficulty with all of the Reformation eucharistic theologies is that they are preoccupied with the question of space: How can Christ's risen body be in heaven and at the same time in the eucharistic loaf? Behind this are two crucial (and from our perspective questionable) assumptions: (1) that heaven is a defined geographical place—presumably somewhere above the known universe; (2) that the risen body of Christ has a physicality akin to (though not necessarily identical with) a resuscitated and levitated corpse.

Current affirmations about the resurrection of the Lord (not to be confused with denials of it) rest on very different assumptions. Therefore eucharistic theologies appropriate to our assumptions must be constructed; otherwise contemporary faith will not seek, let alone find, any suitable understanding. But we cannot let this urgent current reality blind us to the importance of medieval and Reformation eucharistic theology. These are the background out of which we now work, and we can learn much both from their values and from their limitations.

Above all, if the old answers no longer work, still the old reasons for wrestling with the issues are there; and in eucharistic theology the basic issue is that of grace and faith. Is the Supper of the Lord a primary means of grace that can increase our faith, or is it simply a way of expressing and perhaps of buttressing the faith we already have? This question of sacrament versus ordinance, which divided Luther and Calvin from the Zwinglians, is as pertinent now as it was in the sixteenth century. If the Supper is indeed a divine gift—Christ's feast with the church—surely its capacity for increasing faith must be taken seriously.

Faith is a positive human response to divine goodness. Of the many ways in which that goodness can be made known to us, the breaking of the bread in the midst of the congregation of Christ's people is one very clearly commended to us: commanded in scripture, examined by theologians from Paul to the present, attested by the practice of the centuries, and experienced by a great cloud of witnesses too venerable to ignore. This feast—so commanded, examined, attested, and experienced—we enjoy in *anamnesis* of Christ, that nourished by divine grace we may grow and bear fruit.

CHAPTER FOUR

# FROM AGE TO AGE

The familiar English translation of Luther's most famous Reformation hymn asserts that Christ is "from age to age the same." However cogent the assertion may be with respect to the true Host of the eucharistic feast, it is far less applicable to the way in which the feast itself has been observed, for the history of eucharistic practice is kaleidoscopic. We can touch here only on major trends—and then primarily on those that help us to understand our own situation and current programs of eucharistic reform.

The Supper of the Lord as a full congregational meal, clearly the practice at Corinth, may or may not have been universal at first. Certainly such a practice was not sustained long, and probably for very practical reasons.

First, except where congregations are quite small, having a common meal once a week becomes logistically difficult. Many congregations in our day have some form of "coffee hour" or "tea" as a part of Sunday fellowship each week, but how well would these same parishes manage a complete meal each Sunday? Furthermore, a full meal assumes both ample time and freedom of movement. Both of these became significant problems for the church as it moved into the Roman world, particularly in times of persecution, when Christians could not own places of worship and often met in secrecy.

Second, Christians insisted on worshiping once every seven days. The church shifted this firm Jewish practice from the seventh day of the week (commemorating the Exodus out of Egypt and the completion of creation) to the first day of the week (celebrating the new Exodus out of sin and death and the new creation inaugurated in the resurrection of Christ). Christians understood this "Lord's Day" to be the fulfillment, not the overthrow, of their Judaic weekly commemoration. In the Roman calendar there was not a holiday once every seven days; so, for the most part, Christians had to worship either very early in the morning before the work day began, or after returning home from work in the evening. Neither practice lent itself to a full communal meal every week. We have already seen the problems in Corinth, where the wealthy, with their flexible schedules, arrived early in the evening, while the working classes could not come until later.

Hence the reduction of a full meal to a token rite. Even so, while exact practices varied from time to time and place to place, the characteristic eucharistic acts were preserved throughout the ancient church. Our best clues to early practice in the post-New Testament period come from two authors: Justin Martyr and Hippolytus.[1]

## THE TESTIMONIES OF JUSTIN MARTYR AND HIPPOLYTUS

Around A.D. 150 Justin, a believer who later would be martyred, wrote a description of Christian worship to prevent misunderstanding among those whose opinions of Christianity were based on hearsay, for damaging rumors filled the Roman world. Because it was known that worshipers drank wine and exchanged a "kiss of peace"—men with men and women with women—it was supposed that Christian worship included drunken homosexual orgies. And because it was known that the faithful shared in eating "the body of Christ," it was also reported that Christianity was a cannibalistic cult. Justin therefore set forth a simple and straightforward description of what in fact did occur in the liturgy of the church.

Justin notes first the importance of communal worship: All Christians gather together on the Lord's Day. Once assembled, there are readings from what today we call the Old and New Testaments, "as time allows." (Here is an intimation that when the service is held in the evening or on a day that is a civil holiday, the service can be longer than on the morning of a work day.) Then, says Justin, the one who presides delivers a discourse and exhortation based on the writings—that is, preaches a sermon relating the passages just read to Christian faith and life. Next there are prayers, the people standing (following traditional synagogue practice). Thus far we have what to many Protestants today is familiar as the basic form of the Sunday "preaching service."

Then, reports Justin, the one who presides receives the gifts of bread and wine and give thanks to God. The people conclude the prayer with their word of assent, "Amen" (another evidence of the Jewishness of the ancient church even after its Hellenization). Next everyone partakes of the bread and wine. That is the basic outline of the Eucharist as we know it still today.

Finally, Justin notes, the remaining bread and wine are carried by deacons (servers) to those who could not attend the service (presumably due to incapacity or even, perhaps, because work schedules would not permit) and those who are able give an offering, which the presider distributes to all in need—specifically mentioned, in good biblical tradition, are orphans and widows, the sick, the imprisoned, and strangers sojourning in the community.

An insistent corporate sense pervades Justin's account: (1) All who are able are to gather on Sunday. Worship is not optional; it is central to what it means to be the church. Those who for good reason cannot attend are not thereby excluded; the bread and wine are carried to them so they may share with the rest of the congregation in the Lord's Day observance. (2) All worshipers are to stand up to offer intercessions together after the sermon, and to join in the unison "Amen" after the prayer of the one who presides at table. (3) Justin specifically notes that everyone partakes of bread and wine; it is a matter of communal action, not personal option. (4) The sharing of an offering with any in need seals the sense of community care and responsibility. Thus throughout Justin's account there is a strong sense of the congregation—not the individual—as the irreducible unit of Christianity.

It is helpful here to note how far contemporary understanding is out of line with these four assumptions:

(1) It is by no means taken for granted today that each Sunday all Christians should be united in the liturgy. Thus in most of our congregations the proposal set forth in chapter 7 that we reinstitute the taking of communion from the congregation to those who for good reason cannot attend will likely be deemed not only novel but unnecessary. Let the pastor give communion to shut-ins on Thursday afternoon, or whenever else is convenient, without regard for the timing of the parish Eucharist. And those whose Sunday work schedules do not permit them to attend will have to fend for themselves as best they can.

(2) Similarly strange to our day is the ancient understanding of common prayer. Many Protestants are accustomed only to a form of intercession in which the worshiper, in effect, eavesdrops on the "pastoral prayer" of the clergy, and sees no reason as to why even the word *amen* should be spoken in unison as a means of ratifying the words spoken by a leader on behalf of all present. Nor does it strike many today as odd that "amens" are added to hymns that, having been sung by the entire congregation, need no such ratification. We view the "amen" more as a concluding ornament than as a corporate ratification by the body of the faithful gathered around the Table of the Lord on the Lord's Day in the Lord's House.

(3) The decision whether or not to receive the bread and wine is viewed today almost entirely as an individual matter; many thus elect not to receive, and may indeed stay home entirely on eucharistic occasions. Even that civil sense of families needing to gather at a common board for Thanksgiving or Christmas dinner seems to have little corollary in the contemporary church. Today eating and drinking with the Lord are viewed as being a matter of choice, but in Justin's time it was seen as being a matter of church; all who form the body of Christ are together to be nourished and strengthened for their common ministry.

(4) Certainly the ancient understanding of offering has been ruined in our time by concerns that are almost exclusively pragmatic. An offering is received because there are parish bills

to be paid, not because caring for those in need is part and parcel of eucharistic sharing. Rarely today is the offering seen as a necessary expression of the concern of the church both for the unity of all its members and for the welfare of the whole of creation, as believers seek to enact here the reality hoped for in heaven. Indeed, many worshipers today would think the ancient reasons for taking an offering to be suspiciously reminiscent of socialism, if not outright communism.

In many instances, the charitable work of our congregations is supported not through the principal Sunday offering but by "special" offerings, personal donations to funds outside the church budget or fund-raising projects, such as bazaars and bake sales. Even when the regular church budget does laudably include line items for the hungry, the homeless, and the like, these are usually minuscule amounts in comparison to the items for salaries, building maintenance, and "church" work. In some places, on communion Sunday a second offering (usually designated "for the poor") is solicited. Here may be some connection, at least, to the ancient understanding that those with whom the Lord shares in the eucharistic feast then share with all whom the Lord has created. But the tenuousness of this connection is seen in the common complaint that taking such an offering "makes it seem like we are being asked to pay for receiving communion."

Thus the contemporary church has much to comprehend about the nature of the church and of Christian mission before its understanding of the eucharistic feast can be as rich as that of the second century. Fortunately the traffic flows both ways, so that the feast, already in place, can provide us with a richer understanding of church and mission than we now have—if only great care is given to perceive and share that understanding.

While Justin describes the second-century service, he provides no text of the rite. The first extensive text we have comes from Hippolytus around A.D. 215; but likely it reflects what was practiced fifty years or so earlier, very close to Justin's own time. Hippolytus was resisting changes already occurring in Rome in his day, and likely reported not what happened in 215 so much as what he wished still were happening then.[2]

Describing a Eucharist presided over by a bishop, Hippolytus reports this dialogue at the beginning of the prayer:

Bishop: The Lord be with you.
People: And with your spirit.
Bishop: Up with your hearts.
People: We have (them) with the Lord.
Bishop: Let us give thanks to the Lord.
People: It is fitting and right.

Hippolytus then gives an example of a eucharistic prayer, which

a. recounts God's goodness, particularly in the coming of Jesus Christ;
b. incorporates the Words of Institution of the Supper;
c. offers the bread and wine to God in remembrance of the Lord's death and resurrection;
d. asks for the gift of the Holy Spirit upon both the offering of the eucharistic elements and upon those who will receive them;
e. prays for the unity of the church and the effectiveness of its witness;
f. concludes with a Trinitarian doxology.

Except for the lack of a *Sanctus* ["Holy, holy, holy Lord . . . "] and a *Benedictus qui venit* ["Blessed is He who comes . . . "] between (a) and (b), it is a pattern well known to us. In tone the prayer is exalted and deals with cosmic realities, including future expectation; sentimentality and individualistic pietism are absent.

Given the proximity in history of the descriptive outline of the liturgy from Justin and an actual liturgical text from Hippolytus, several things are striking: (1) In the second century the church had clearly established patterns and forms of worship. (2) These were consistent with the Jewish heritage and New Testament witness. (3) These are familiar to us, though the contemporary understanding of their meaning may be different.

On the third point: Not only have many recently revised

liturgies been heavily influenced by Hippolytus, but also much of the language he used was preserved in both medieval and post-Reformation formularies and in later adaptations in common use. The average congregation of Catholics, Lutherans, Anglicans, Methodists, or Presbyterians today, hearing a felicitous contemporary translation of the Hippolytan prayer, will have little sense of novelty or disorientation with respect to wording; but the same congregation is apt to have lost much of the corporate and cosmic meaning characteristic of the ancient era. The words, while familiar, are likely understood in an individualistic way alien to the first and second centuries; in particular the original eschatological overtones likely either will be missed or reinterpreted in terms of personal salvation alone.

How then are we to respond to these ancient reports of eucharistic worship? We cannot return to the distant past in some romantic way; nor do we believe that new interpretations are automatically evidence of degeneration. (Otherwise what do we mean by asserting that the Holy Spirit is at work in every age, ever seeking to teach the church new ways of being and doing?) Still, we must face the fact that Justin and Hippolytus were very significantly closer to the apostolic age than we are. And given the remarkable Jewish character of the practices of these authors in Gentile Rome, they cannot have strayed terribly far from what they had inherited from the New Testament church so few decades earlier.[3] It is foolish for us to dismiss the practices of Justin and Hippolytus as irrelevant relics of Christian antiquity—as foolish as it would be for us to attempt to copy them exactly in our parishes now. A tension between appreciation and adaptation is crucial.

## THE CHANGING SCENE IN THE EARLY CENTURIES

In the course of the first four or five centuries of the Christian era, practices and understandings were altered as local circumstances and social forces dictated. Persecution ceased with Constantine's Peace of the Church (A.D. 313), and Sunday became a civil holiday, thus allowing ample time for the Lord's

Day service. Security precautions at worship services, often mandatory in times of persecution, became unnecessary. The church could own property, which earlier had been illegal. In fact, Constantine himself and his devout mother, Helena, contributed liberally toward the construction of church buildings. Thus impressive edifices were erected, choirs formed, and elaborate ceremonies introduced in keeping with what was deemed to be appropriate for public functions in that era.

Constantine granted to bishops and other church officials insignia and perquisites previously reserved for civic dignitaries. Ultimately the emperor left Rome to live in Byzantium (renamed Constantinople in his honor); the church was then called upon to provide a sense of continuity in the former capital by adapting and preserving the protocol of the departed imperial court. In short, the liturgy accumulated to itself many things that had little to do with the basic worship practices of the church in its first two centuries. Yet throughout the period immediately after Constantine, those basic practices seem to have survived. Even as assumptions about the nature of the church and Christianity's role in society were altered, the service of scripture with sermon and prayer culminating in the Eucharist was a weekly corporate experience for the baptized.

The unbaptized were to attend the service, to listen to the scriptures and the sermon, and then to depart; until they were full members of the community, they could not pray with the company of believers nor could they join in the family meal of the faithful.[4] Instead they attended separate sessions with those who directed their growth in the faith; these sessions continued for as long as three years prior to baptism. Yet throughout all that period these learners did not receive the Eucharist, nor even hear it described in any detail, as best we know. Nor did they pray the central prayer of the church or know its basic creed. Only the week before their baptism were they taught the Lord's Prayer and the Apostles' Creed; only after their baptism did they receive the bread and wine. Each day of the week following, they came to church and had explained to them the meaning of these new practices.

All of this seems incredibly odd to us. We are accustomed to worship so thoroughly public that someone utterly unfamiliar with Christianity can attend any of our services and observe everything; indeed some congregations would view it as an inhospitable gesture not to invite such a stranger to join in the prayers, if not the creed and communion. And certainly no communion servers inquire of strangers who present themselves at the Lord's Table, "Are you baptized?"—even though their liturgies may include a statement of invitation that specifically indicates the Eucharist is for the baptized.

Alien and exclusivistic though they may seem, do these ancient practices at least convey to us our loss of a sense of "churchness"? Without seeking to recover such early practices as dismissing the unbaptized, do we at least need to ask how we can restore the reality that Christ's feast is a family meal that looks to the future for its fulfillment? The church is not a cafeteria with separate booths and tables at which individuals who have little in common dine in isolation, hoping only to have personal needs met thereby. Perhaps in a much greater way than we realize, we have forfeited the conviction that those who eat together are bound together, that when we break the bread we share in the body of Christ and anticipate our feast with Christ and the saints at the end of time.

Some important reasons as to why we have lost that conviction lie in the next several periods of church history.

## THE MIDDLE AGES

In the fourth century, Augustine found it useful to develop a very hard-nosed concept of sin in his battle against that congenitally optimistic monk, Pelagius. In subsequent centuries, Augustine's grim ideas became the foundation for an elaborate superstructure of doctrine, which can be summarized as follows.

The atoning work of Christ upon the cross is sacramentally transmitted to individuals through baptism, thus removing the awful consequences imposed by that stain inherited by each of us from Adam and Eve. (This stain is usually called "original sin" though "original guilt" would be more accurate.) Baptism must be administered as soon after birth as practical, for without it even infants cannot enter heaven but are eternally consigned to the shadowy nothingness known as "limbo."

Although the inherited stain is removed, all people beyond early childhood commit sin through their own actions. This "actual sin" also incurs the wrath of a just God. Some few may lead lives of such utter faith and good works as to cancel out their actual sins; at death these rare individuals may well enter heaven immediately. But what about the rest of us? The rest of us, it turns out, must pay for our sins before we can attain bliss. Hence there is purgatory—a time (and presumably a place) of purgation where we can make up for whatever sins we have willfully committed after baptism but have not counteracted by righteous living.

As descriptions of the agonies of purgatory became more vivid, and as anxiety about the time to be spent there increased, it was natural for people to want to find some way of shortening the sentence. This desire was readily accommodated in a variety of ways, one of which was disastrous for earlier understandings of eucharistic worship. The disaster lay in the idea that the Eucharist is a propitiatory sacrifice; this sacrifice on the altar, offered in the name of a Christian in purgatory, reduces the time of confinement and thus hastens the entry of the deceased person into heaven.

This system of eucharistic sacrifice in exchange for diminished suffering seems utterly fantastic until we connect it with the view of reality and the resulting doctrines of eucharistic Presence discussed in chapter 3. Simply grant that bread and wine become the body and blood of Christ (whether by means of Extreme or Moderate Realism); then it is an easy step to the notion that when the bread is broken and the wine poured upon the altar, the events of Calvary are not only re-enacted but carry with them a force like that of the historical crucifixion itself. If the benefits of the atonement achieved when the body of Christ was broken on the cross can counteract original sin, then why cannot the benefits of the atonement achieved when the body of Christ is broken on the altar cancel out actual sin?

Such reasoning provides an appealing way out of purgatory. Have Masses offered in your name after your death, and each Mass will reduce the length of your punishment. But these Masses are not free—a fee is to be paid for each one so offered. Rarely have human anxiety about salvation in the future and ecclesiastical anxiety about fund raising in the present so fully coincided, to the apparent benefit of both parties! The affluent shortly discovered they could endow Masses to be said perpetually for themselves or family members. The very wealthy even paid for the addition to large church buildings of private chapels (called "chantries") in which such endowed Masses could be offered daily for themselves and their deceased relatives and friends.

Soon the demand for Masses far exceeded the number of priests available. Because a priest normally was restricted to one full Mass and personal communion per day, there arose the abuse known as "the dry Mass." The priest needed to offer, let us say, eight propitiatory Masses on a given morning. Seven times he read his way through the formulary right up to the point of consecrating the bread and wine, then backed up and started over; only the eighth time did he complete the rite. Furthermore, all of this the priest had to do on a fasting stomach—that is, before breakfast (hence our word for the meal that "breaks the fast"). The rate at which the hungry priest worked his way through seven "dry" Masses on his way to the full Mass is not difficult to imagine.

Envision now an ample cathedral or monastic church with a large contingent of clergy in residence. On a given day, each of thirty-seven priests, let us say, will need to say half a dozen Masses. The church has twenty altars, so two shifts must be completed before the entire religious community can share a communal breakfast in the refectory. While seventeen more impatiently wait their turn, twenty priests simultaneously race through Latin liturgies in a very reverberent Romanesque building with high stone vaulting. The resulting cacophony dictates that rather than speaking or chanting in a clearly audible voice, the priests shall use hushed tones, sometimes whispering the Mass or even falling totally silent. There is no congregation present on most days, so it matters little if anyone hears. Nor could most worshipers understand if they did hear, since knowledge of Latin is the preserve of the well-educated.[5]

On Sundays or at other times when the congregation attends, the faithful function largely as spectators. For it becomes customary on ordinary occasions for Mass to be said according to the form known as "Low Mass"—without a choir in attendance and with a reduced amount of ceremonial action.

While in ancient times the celebrant faced the congregation across the Lord's Table, it later became the practice for the priest to stand with his back toward the congregation. This came to be justified by asserting that it enhanced the sense of mystery, since the people could not then see exactly what was being done, or that the priest stood as a mediator between the worshiper and God. The practice may have originated, however, because the priest literally could no longer see over the top of the ornate holy objects that had come to clutter the back of the eucharistic table.[6]

Envision now the medieval Sunday situation. During the beginning of the service, the people arrive at various times and mill about the building. They cannot hear most of what is being said (or whispered) by the priest, let alone comprehend Latin, were it audible. They occupy themselves by looking at the scenes depicted in stained glass or the carved stations of the cross along the walls. Those who are both literate and affluent may bring with them a personal prayer book from which to read; others may engage in a memorized course of prayers, using rosary beads to guide them. There is little congregational seating, except perhaps for some benches around the walls to accommodate those who cannot tolerate long stretches of standing or kneeling.

At length a server at the altar rings a bell. The worshipers know the signal and drop reverently to their knees. The moment of "the miracle" is about to occur. This is why they have come—to see the mystery of ordinary bread and wine become the body and blood of their Lord. Out of reverence, perhaps even fear (since one had to be cleansed of sin by confession and penance before presenting oneself for the bread) they will not partake of communion except at Easter—and under constraint of church law even then.[7]

The bell at the altar rings again. The priest says (perhaps now loudly enough to be heard by everyone) words that are familiar, even if their translation into the vernacular is not known: *Hoc est enim corpus meum* ("For this is my body"). As the bell is rung thrice, to signal the congregation of this most holy action, the priest genuflects deeply before the sacred bread, arises, and (with his back still to the people) lifts the sacred wafer high above his head so that all may see it. He replaces the bread on the table and again bows deeply. Then corresponding words and actions are repeated with the chalice. The people continue to kneel reverently until another bell releases them. They have seen what they came to see; if they did not, because the priest was inept, they may have called out (as is reported to have happened in England): "Hold it higher, Sir Priest, so we can see the miracle."

Those well schooled in the liturgy knew that they were also to see past the miracle on the altar to that which it repeated: the saving action on Calvary. Numerous artists portrayed both events—the crucifixion and the consecration of the host—on the same canvas to help the people understand. Further, there was developed an entire mental regimen in which worshipers could engage, known as the "allegorical Mass." Each action of the priest represented an event in the biblical passion narrative; at the very beginning, for example, when the priest first ascended the altar stairs, the faithful were to envision Jesus walking up the staircase of the house of Pontius Pilate to face judgment and sentencing.

Because the Mass was seen as an effective sacrifice for actual sin, eucharistic theology and action became fixated at Calvary to the virtual exclusion of all else, making the rite increasingly somber. Artists, for example, depicted the celebrating priest weeping as he broke the consecrated bread—for this action allegorically represented the Savior's death, and it should elicit emotions commensurate with that sorrowful event.

Note carefully what did not happen during the medieval eucharistic rite. There was virtually no corporate congregational prayer, except perhaps the saying of the Lord's Prayer, which the people were supposed to have memorized. Nor was there congregational singing; even when music was used, it was sung in Latin by a choir carefully trained in the intricacies of the Gregorian chant. Above all, except on special occasions, there was no sermon. Contrary to popular belief (particularly among Protestants) preaching did not disappear during the Middle Ages; but divorced from the Eucharist, it was done at other times, often by clergy other than the parish priest.[8]

The belief that the bread and wine became the body and blood of the Lord in a very corporeal way gave rise to various practices unknown in the ancient church. At the close of Mass, the priest must drink all of the wine and then cleanse the chalice carefully, lest any trace remain. Should the consecrated wine accidentally be spilled, specific rites for its removal were required. Because spillage could occur so readily when administering the cup to the communicant, it became the practice that only the officiating priest drank the wine. All others received the bread only.[9]

Even the bread had to be administered in a particular way, lest the wafer be dropped as it was transferred from one person to another. So it became the practice for the priest to place the sacred bread directly upon the extended tongue of the communicant; meanwhile, an acolyte or server held a tray under the chin of the recipient, lest the wafer be accidentally dropped or ejected. The faithful were taught to swallow the bread whole, for by chewing they would manducate the body of Christ in an impious manner.

Bread that was not eaten could not be thrown away but was to be "reserved" for a variety of uses: (1) communion outside of Mass, particularly as it was distributed to the sick and dying; (2) special corporate reverencing, in services of "the exposition and benediction of the Blessed Sacrament" or processions with the sacred bread on occasions such as the Feast of Corpus Christi; (3) private acts of devotion, in which worshipers would use the place of reservation as a focus for personal prayer and adoration; (4) distribution at Mass itself; if more communicants presented themselves than had been provided for in the consecration of bread on that day, rather than repeat the act of consecration the priest would make up the deficit from the reserved sacrament.

Since often the consecrated bread was reserved for long periods, ordinary leavened bread was unsuitable, though it had been used in the ancient church, as it still is in Eastern Orthodoxy. Therefore, unleavened wafers were used, since they took up less space and were subject neither to dehydration nor to putrefaction. But by being unlike household bread, and therefore "special," the wafer made the Eucharist seem even further removed from a true meal than it had been made to seem by its necessary reduction from a full repast to a token rite.

Because it was so sacred, the reserved bread was stored in a locked receptacle, such as a "tabernacle," based on a literal translation of John 1:14: "The Word became flesh and tabernacled among us." A candle known as the "sanctuary lamp" identified the site of the reserved sacrament, located on or near at the main altar, but sometimes at a separate altar or in a "sacrament house" or even in a reservation chapel. Devout Christians, before walking past the reserved bread, genuflected reverently and even might have doffed the hat when passing the exterior of the building, out of respect for the sacramental body of the Lord. Between Good Friday and the first Mass of Easter Day, the reserved bread was removed from its usual container, whose door was left open, with the identifying lamp extinguished, and was taken to a separate "altar of repose" representing the sepulcher of Jesus—all to signal the grief of the church awaiting the liturgical observance of the resurrection. Nor was any bread and wine consecrated on Good Friday; on that day the church remembered the death of the Lord in a particularly somber way.

Public services of adoration and festival processions of the sacrament occasioned the use of a "monstrance"—an ornate vessel with a circular, hinged glass door slightly larger than the diameter of a communion wafer. A consecrated wafer inserted behind the door became a focal point for veneration. Often the monstrance was in the form of a sunburst, with the sacred wafer being the "sun."

No matter how repugnant these eucharistic practices came to be to Protestants determined to reform them, the observances were not totally superstitious but had deep meaning for many sophisticated believers; indeed, some of the practices preserved affirmations of the resurrection that tended to get lost in the emphasis on the daily Mass as a sacrifice on behalf of those in purgatory. The reserved sacrament was seen as a form of resurrected presence of the Lord in the church. The sunburst monstrance revealed this risen One to be the light of the world, the fulfillment of the promise that "the sun of righteousness shall rise, with healing in its wings" (Mal. 4:2). And the particular practices surrounding Good Friday intensified the understanding of the death and entombment of the Lord.

But a serious problem is implied in the phrase "sophisticated believers" at the beginning of the paragraph above. Such Christians were an elite group, confined largely to the clergy, and mostly to the scholars among them. Others could not grasp the subtleties of Moderate or Extreme Realism; for them the sacrament was the literal, physical body of the Jesus of history in a way that engendered superstition. Aside from the danger of dropping it, there was another reason why the consecrated wafer came to be placed directly on the tongue of the communicants. In the absence of this practice, unsophisticated worshipers had been known not to place the bread in their mouths after it was handed to them, but to slip it into a pocket and take it home for other use; there it might be saved and taken as a medication in time of grave illness, rubbed against persons or objects as a way of blessing or protecting them, or even consumed as an aphrodisiac. Similarly, the sophisticated might understand that the prohibition against chewing the wafer was not to be taken to mean that this bread was the same flesh of the Jesus who walked on earth during the incarnation. But try explaining that to an untutored serf, or even to someone of much higher station who lacked training in philosophy!

The esoteric character of medieval Platonic and Aristotelian thought inexorably produced gross superstition among ordinary people, and the propitiatory sacrifice of the Mass for shortening time in purgatory unavoidably resulted in gross abuse at a practical level—despite the good intentions of the theologians in both instances.

Given the medieval situation, is it any wonder that the

Reformers were distressed and even indignant as they evaluated what they had inherited? Their sometimes outlandish verbal abuse of the papacy, and their often extreme remedies, must be assessed in the context of what has been set forth above. To that assessment, and to what later generations made of it, we now turn.

## THE REACTION OF THE REFORMERS

Considering the seriousness of the situation, it would hardly be remarkable to find the Reformers acting decisively, or even overreacting in their zeal to correct medieval abuses of the Eucharist.[10] What is remarkable is the slowness of Luther to change the liturgy. He had issued his ninety-five points of dispute with the church in 1517, but it was more than six years before he made changes in the Mass, and even these were conservative. It was not that he saw nothing wrong. Both in preaching and in his writing (particularly in *The Babylonian Captivity of the Church* in 1520), Luther criticized theological abuse of the liturgy; still, he found in the Mass a source of stability and order he felt it well to maintain, lest his followers feel that everything they valued religiously was being mutilated, or even destroyed all at once. He understood that religious conviction can produce an emotional attachment to the familiar liturgy—be it good or bad—and that this attachment should be treated gingerly.

As early as 1521, when Luther was in hiding in Wartburg Castle, his associate in Wittenberg, Andreas Carlstadt, instituted reforms in the service; but Luther was unhappy with the pace and extent of the changes. He feared (probably rightly) that the faith of simple folk would be shattered if they did not understand why practices they had known all their lives suddenly were abolished. So in December of 1523 Luther published *Formula Missae* (*Form of the Mass*), a more reasoned and less drastic set of reforms than those of Carlstadt.

Luther retained Latin in the service except for the inclusion in German of hymns and the sermon; the latter, he strongly insisted, must be an integral part of Mass, not something optional or detached. He abolished all parts of the rite that reinforced the offensive idea of the Eucharist's being a propitiatory sacrifice for souls in purgatory. Private Masses by the priest were forbidden as pointless. The Eucharist is a community act, the Reformer insisted; therefore, it must not be celebrated unless there are laity to receive, and to receive "in both kinds"—the cup as well as the bread. Finally, Luther continued the practice of confession, seeing it as a useful way of achieving the examination of heart he deemed crucial for a right reception of the sacrament.

Two years later, Luther made further changes when he published his *Deutsche Messe* (German Mass). As the name suggests, a text now was provided in the vernacular. But Luther not only still permitted a revised Latin text; he even wished that the service could be said and sung in German, Latin, Greek, and Hebrew on successive Sundays! This he suggested both for the sake of "the youth" (who studied these languages in school, often without having any practical application for them) and with an eye to preventing provincialism.[11]

The 1526 revision specifically retained the use of vestments and such things as the crucifix and candles, which his more radical associates had urged him to abolish. Luther called such things *adiaphora*; while this often is translated as "indifferent," such a rendering is unduly negative. His point was that some things can be usefully employed in situations where they are edifying, yet discarded under circumstances where they are impediments to piety. Thus they are neither to be rejected as repugnant nor mandated as essential. This solid pastoral insight is as applicable in our day as it was in Luther's time.

Closely related was a Reformation dispute about the relationship between acceptable practices and biblical injunction. The more radical Reformers believed that if the Bible does not specifically command (or at least allow) a certain practice, it is forbidden to the church. But Luther asserted that if the Bible does not specifically forbid a certain practice, it is allowable for the church. This difference (over what is called "biblical warrant") is a watershed that still causes disputes in the contemporary church.

In his 1526 statement, Luther suggested (but did not insist) that the pastor stand facing the congregation across the Lord's Table, so that the people could see more than the back of the celebrant and could experience a greater sense of community. German hymns were more fully integrated into the service in 1526 than they had been in 1523.

Luther observed that the Sunday congregation necessarily will consist of those who attend because of custom and social pressure as well as the truly devout ("those who mean to be real Christians, and profess the Gospel with hand and mouth," as he described the latter). Although he did not yet think the time ripe, Luther hoped that one day the more serious Christians might meet in home fellowship groups as the *ecclesiolae in ecclesia,* the "little churches within the church." We will see shortly how this idea backfired on later generations of Lutherans in the movement known as Pietism.

While we think of Luther as a radical (primarily because he was the first and best-known of the sixteenth-century Reformers), his liturgical principles were conservative; he firmly held that abuse does not prevent the continued use of a practice. (*Abusus non tollit usum* is the formal statement of that principle.) Voices to the left argued that if a practice has resulted in gross abuse it must be abolished. Luther preferred to reinterpret a distorted practice except when its foundational assumptions were clearly repugnant. Hence priestly vestments, festival days, and chanting were maintained in Lutheranism, while propitiatory Masses by a solitary priest were abolished. More important, the Eucharist was reaffirmed as a sacrament of the Lord's risen Presence, while the doctrine of transubstantiation was abolished.

Of the three major Reformers, Zwingli was the radical in revising the rites, as in rejecting any teaching about Presence. He was much more determined than Luther to find biblical warrant for medieval practices before retaining them, though he also was something of a gradualist in instituting reform.

At Zurich, Zwingli made minor changes in the Mass in 1523, primarily to rid it of its character as a propitiatory sacrifice for those in purgatory. The following year he instituted reforms that highlighted his disagreement with Luther over *abusus non tollit usum.* Zwingli rid the churches of statuary, paintings, and crosses, and he locked the pipe organs, declaring that never again should their music be heard. Only the Word of God should be listened to in church! Even unaccompanied congregational singing was abolished in favor of responsive speaking between men and women. (Luther, meanwhile, was busy composing new hymns for his flock.)

Zwingli was ever under constraint from even more radical reformers to his left: the Anabaptists. (They were dubbed this because they rejected the baptism of the medieval church as invalid and insisted on baptizing "again," as Luther and other opponents interpreted it; they themselves insisted they were baptizing for the first time, since the medieval rite amounted to no baptism at all.) Responding to this pressure, in 1525 Zwingli abolished the Mass. The usual Sunday service now was based on the medieval service called "prone," an order centered on preaching, with prayer and related acts.

A commemorative service of the Passion of the Lord was to be held four times a year (Easter, Pentecost, autumn, and Christmas) using the bread and cup, but no longer was this to be seen as a communication of grace from God to the people to elicit faith. Rather, it was an affirmation of devotion from the people to God, in expression of their faith. Still, on all Sundays Zwingli used a fixed order of service, about which the Anabaptists were unhappy. They agreed with Zwingli on theological interpretation, but liturgically they preferred to leave as much as possible to the spontaneity of the moment.[12]

Zwingli specified in the preface to his eucharistic order that plates and cups were to be made of wood rather than jewel-encrusted gold, in order that medieval "pomp may not come back again." At Easter, at least, he segregated communicants by age. The youth were to receive on Holy Thursday, the middle-aged on Good Friday, and the elderly on Easter Day, with males and females being separated from each other in all instances. It is difficult to know whether his reasons were theological or merely practical and cultural. Did he reason

(1) that the inconstancy of the disciples on Thursday night would be a good moral lesson on faithfulness to Christ for young people? (2) That the middle-aged, having had ample opportunity to know temptation and sin, would resonate more fully with the atonement theme of Friday? (3) And that the elderly, approaching death, could benefit most from the hope of resurrection set forth on Sunday? Or did Zwingli simply consider all days to be alike and divide people up for other reasons entirely? It is by no means clear.

Calvin was only thirteen years old when Luther and Zwingli made their initial eucharistic reforms of 1523. In his maturity, then, Calvin benefited from the experimentation and experience of the generation before him. He was greatly influenced by the reforms of Martin Bucer, with whom he worked in Strassburg and who in turn had been influenced by both Luther and Zwingli (though more strongly by the former). It was less necessary for Calvin to make innovations than to adapt what others had done before him. His primary contribution is in the arena of liturgical theology, not practice.

Like Luther, Calvin insisted on retaining the Lord's Supper as a sacrament and on reestablishing preaching as a central component of the weekly service. Also like Luther, he wanted the Eucharist weekly, but neither Reformer was able to establish this for the simple reason that people will not begin to do willingly once a week what they have done only once a year, and then under constraint of church law. Calvin did, however, institute monthly communions in Geneva and established the schedule so that the sacrament was celebrated each Sunday in at least one of the churches; thus those who wanted a weekly Eucharist could simply itinerate from one congregation to another. This practical compromise was both gain and loss; weekly reception could be attained at the cost of cohesive congregational life.

Unlike Zwingli, Calvin highly valued congregational singing; but unlike Luther, he did not care for newly devised hymn texts. Therefore, he instituted the singing of the biblical psalms only, though these were paraphrased and adjusted to poetic meter so they could be sung to hymn tunes rather than needing to be a chanted use of a strict translation of the Hebrew text.

Only once various reform movements were well under way on the Continent did the Reformation take hold in the British Isles. In England, *The Book of Common Prayer* as it was first issued in 1549 by Archbishop Thomas Cranmer was deemed by many to be too "Catholic" in both theology and practice. Hence a more drastic revision was represented by the 1552 *Book of Common Prayer*. Even so, both books assumed a Sunday eucharistic order as the norm. When that failed in practice, the preaching service used instead was not an adaptation of the eucharistic rite without an actual celebration of the Supper. Rather illogically, the preaching order came to be the service of Morning Prayer with a sermon appended.

Morning Prayer, being a daily office, was not designed to include preaching, and its adaptation for this purpose had a less than happy outcome that Cranmer could not have foreseen. At the Eucharist, the sermon was preached immediately after the scriptures were read, thus encouraging biblical preaching. But with the scriptures read early in Morning Prayer (following a daily lectionary, not the weekly one designated for Eucharist) and with the sermon tacked on at the end, the link between reading and exposition was broken. Further, because the two orders were quite different in their arrangement, and because Morning Prayer became the more familiar of the two due to its frequency, the eucharistic order often came to be regarded as an oddity or intrusion on "the way we usually do things." This problem is well known today in churches that have the sacrament only infrequently and then use a rite very different from the usual Sunday preaching service; this is one reason why recently revised orders seek to follow the same basic pattern Sunday by Sunday, whether the sacrament is celebrated or not.

To recapitulate, it should be said that all of the liturgical reform movements worked primarily in reaction to what immediately preceded their own time. The revisers had far less access to documents of the earlier periods than we do today, so their reforms were guided not so much by a knowledge of historical development and distortion as by liturgical intuition and by theological disputes within the church of their age. Attempts to reform twentieth-century liturgy by copying slavishly sixteenth-century patterns can only make our own situation worse.

A case in point: The Reformers (particularly Calvin) were often intolerably long-winded and didactic in their liturgies. Probably they needed to be; people accustomed to coming to church "to see the miracle" in the context of a Latin rite had to be carefully reeducated, and there was little opportunity to do that apart from Sunday morning. But too often this has given Protestants the notion that the primary function of the liturgy is the instruction of the people rather than the glorification of God (through which the people are indeed edified). Even worse, too often the didactic verbosity of Reformation liturgy has resulted in clergy giving an extemporaneous running commentary on the rite every time it is used, or producing printed orders of service that resemble liturgical textbooks rather than simple guides to prayer.[13]

It is also true that in their time the Reformers had to emphasize sincerity rather than custom or church law as the motivation for receiving the Eucharist; and further they had to emphasize that the result of receiving communion is the bearing of fruit rather than the automatic reception of a quantity of saving grace. Hence Luther's insistence on self-examination in his 1523 formulation and Calvin's long exhortations before communion in his rites. (Particularly under the Puritans, the latter evolved into a rigorous "fencing of the Table," which often sought to discourage as many people as possible from receiving the sacrament, lest they "eat and drink unworthily.")

Once such points were established, their repetition came to have a destructive rather than instructive effect. Overly conscientious self-examination resulted in an intensely introspective approach to the sacrament, to say nothing of the conviction imbedded in generation after generation down to our own day that "I am not worthy to receive"—and so will stay at home whenever the Eucharist is celebrated.

## AFTER THE REFORMERS

Our all-too-evident legacy of Reformation teaching gone to seed is the notion that the Lord's Supper is not Christ's feast with the church, but is Christ's reward to deserving individuals within the church. Serious Christians quickly realize that there are few of those around—indeed none, if we take seriously the biblical teaching that salvation is by grace through faith, not by works.

But often we don't take the biblical teaching seriously, which can result in problems of more than one kind. An unexpected manifestation occurred when, in the seventeenth and eighteenth centuries, some German Lutherans took up Luther's musings that perhaps the truly serious Christians should meet for worship in "house churches," separately from the congregation. What started out as services in addition to quickly became services instead of congregational worship. In its worst forms this pietistic movement led to a self-righteous smugness; such separatism seemed to see no value in the New Testament suggestion that the wheat and tares be allowed to grow together in the field until they are sorted by divine discernment at the end of time. Nor were the pietists the last to learn how divisive a force the Eucharist can be when it is seen as the private property of the few—and the "superior" few at that.[14]

Among the Calvinists, subsequent generations were less afflicted with Pietism than with what is often called "Scholasticism"—a hardening of formal doctrine and practice. This was particularly true of the way Calvinists after Calvin came to interpret the doctrine of "election." Only those who with certainty knew themselves to be among the elect of God came to be regarded as fitting communicants. Others might jeopardize their spiritual growth by partaking. Thus the Eucharist came to be preceded by a serious time of self-examination. Often services were held every evening of the week prior to communion Sunday, with the clear expectation that attendance would decrease each succeeding night as more and more realized they were not yet ready to receive. Thus when the sacrament was served, only a small remnant of the congregation partook. The inevitable consequence was that among strict Calvinists the celebrations became more and more infrequent—not because the Eucharist was considered to be unimportant (as among many Zwinglians) but because it was of crucial, but intimidating, import.

Not all ecclesiastical descendants of Calvin were strict Calvinists with respect to the Eucharist, however; the Reformer was more closely followed in the Netherlands and Scotland than in Switzerland, where he had labored so diligently. There the Calvinism of Geneva and the Zwinglianism of Zurich merged to form the established Reformed Church; and sacramentally it was the Zwinglians who tended to have their way.

Elsewhere Zwinglian memorialism also became dominant, ultimately due to the influence of the Age of Reason in the eighteenth century, which saw little point to anything more than an infrequent cerebral remembering of the suffering of that very good teacher and martyr, Jesus of Nazareth. During this era the historic treasures of the church were vandalized in the name of intellectual respectability and anti-clerical hysteria (which was, in part, class-motivated).

Thus in England, a number of individuals rewrote the *Book of Common Prayer* to bring it into line with empirical scientific orthodoxy, including no less a scientist than Joseph Priestly, the discoverer of oxygen. At Notre Dame in Paris, vestments, service books, and religious symbols were cleared away, and the "Goddess of Reason" given place of prominence in their stead; and in America, Thomas Jefferson edited the New Testament, retaining the moral teachings of Jesus but deleting miracle stories and doctrines that presumably had been invented by misguided and superstitious followers of the Galilean.

Against such a popular and prestigious spirit of the times, it was difficult to hold a line—let alone reverse a trend. But in England the Wesleys did just that. When Anglican clergy celebrated the sacrament infrequently (usually only the mandated three times a year: Easter, Pentecost, and Christmas) and Anglican laity attended even less frequently, the Methodists instituted what can only be called a eucharistic revival. On a number of occasions, John Wesley's *Journal* gives reports of more than a thousand and as many as sixteen hundred persons receiving communion at a Methodist service. But the better evidence lies in a singular publication of hymns.[15]

In 1745, Charles and John Wesley published in one volume a set of 166 hymn texts, all on the same subject: the Eucharist. It was no limited edition work, but went through printing after printing. Yet at this time, the Church of England still observed the Calvinistic pattern of using only psalms as congregational songs. So who needed 166 hymns on the Lord's Supper? The Methodist societies that were functioning as renewal groups within the Church of England! At first the texts may have been primarily for edification and instruction in the prayer and study lives of the Methodists, but soon they were sung at the society Eucharists, as hundreds and sometimes thousands were going forward and returning from receiving bread and wine. Indeed the Wesleys wrote more eucharistic hymns than 166; that is simply the number gathered together in a single collection. That collection possibly represents the only time in the entire history of the church that so many poetic texts on the Eucharist were published in one book—let alone primarily by one author (Charles) or with widespread sales.

The eucharistic doctrine in the Wesley hymns is typical of the amalgamated Lutheran-Calvinian liturgical tradition that characterized the English church. The Wesleys affirmed the experience of the eucharistic Presence of Christ, but without any single explanation, or even a sustained attempt to explain. They embrace elements of both Uniquitarianism and Virtualism within their texts—and make many an allusion to or even direct argument against Zwingli's bare Memorialism. Indeed, there are traces in the hymns of the better parts of medieval eucharistic piety; these must have alarmed some Anglicans in the eighteenth century and would astound Methodists today, if only they would study the 166 poems carefully.

But later Methodists rejected the eucharistic piety of their forebears—not so much because they were repulsed by it as that they did not know it and found Zwinglianism more in line with the spirit of the times.[16] But some of the spirit of the Wesleyan eucharistic revival lived on in the Evangelical wing of the Church of England, for in the nineteenth century it was those

Evangelicals who, among the Anglicans, helped to restore an appreciation for the Eucharist.[17]

The post-Reformation period then was one of great alteration in eucharistic piety, engendered in part by the diversity and disagreement within the Reform movement itself and in part by later developments such as pietism, rationalism, and that eroding force common to both—individualism. In recoiling from medieval abuses, the Reformers unknowingly (and certainly unintentionally) set the stage for movement away from rather than toward the eucharistic appreciation of the early centuries of the church. So how is it that there has been a movement back, evident largely within the lifetime of many of us?

## CONTEMPORARY RECONSIDERATION

Since the Second Vatican Council, many Roman Catholics have been heard to mutter after attending Mass that "after four centuries, Rome has decided to capitulate to the Protestants." Meanwhile, many Protestants worry that in their communion practices, "We have become just like the Catholics." And both groups may see this to be the result of some kind of ecumenical conspiracy, or (at best) a silent agreement to "bury the hatchets" so carefully sharpened by both the Reformers and the Counter-Reformation movement following the Council of Trent. The truth lies elsewhere.

Whatever commonality now exists has been achieved largely independently and as the result of complex factors. Among these factors are:

(1) A new respect for biblical materials and meanings. A century ago it was readily believed that along with others Paul, the theological sophisticate, had turned into an elaborate, ritualistic system an ordinary fellowship meal that the simple teacher Jesus had held with twelve followers in an upper room. This transformation (or degeneration) was seen to have more to do with the influence of the Greek mystery religions than with anything imbedded in the Hebraic heritage.

Recent biblical study has reversed the assessment, and a fuller understanding of the church's roots has demonstrated the overwhelming "Jewishness" of early Christianity. Furthermore, recent biblical studies have found eucharistic meanings in New Testament passages that earlier seemed to carry no such weight. (Much of this material is discussed in chapter 2.)

(2) A closer look at the history of the church before the Reformation has resulted in a new regard for the early centuries and a better understanding of what went on in medieval Christianity. Protestants have come to see the positive side of "tradition," which so often had been dismissed as unimportant if not indeed detrimental. The Protestant assumption that the true, vital church died either with the last of the apostles or in the time of Constantine and was recovered by Luther has been exposed as plain error. At the same time, Catholics have come to see that "tradition" is flawed and cannot be relied upon as unerring precedent; the notion that this tradition encased "the Golden Age" of the church has been exposed as romantic fantasy.

(3) Reformation and post-Reformation history has been reassessed on each side of the fence. Both Catholics and Protestants have discovered weaknesses, even distortions, in their sixteenth-century antecedents and what has evolved from them.

(4) Developments in systematic theology have given new attention to the roles of the Holy Spirit, the church, the means of grace, and the experience of the Christian life. There has been a new regard for creation itself as God's activity, not simply as an empty stage upon which God has enacted a divine drama.

(5) Ecumenical contacts have been far less important in negotiating statements of doctrinal agreement to be signed than in establishing dialogue that has revealed a shared faith and facilitated mutual trust. This is true not only for Catholics and Protestants but also of the interaction of both groups with the Orthodox bodies that so long were but shadowy entities to Christians in the West.

(6) As the former mission churches, both Catholic and Protestant, have come into their own, they have both challenged

narrow Western understandings and contributed new patterns of liturgical thought and action. For example, the communal character of much of Christianity in Africa has both judged the individualism of European and American culture and has helped to recover the communal assumptions of biblical thought so often disregarded both by Catholics and by Protestants until recently.

(7) Anthropological and cross-cultural studies have shown not only the relativity of particular forms of liturgy but also the commonality of religious interpretation and expression in a wide variety of settings and eras. This has heightened the role of sacramental rites in society—particularly that of feasting together at crucial junctures in human experience; but at the same time this has reduced the need to establish the "only correct way of doing things," which heretofore tended to plague interdenominational Protestant as well as Catholic-Protestant liturgical discussions.

(8) The assumptions of rationalism and empiricism have been eroded, and nowhere more prominently than within the scientific community. Thoughtful scientists today are less inclined to scoff at the possibility of the sacramentality of the world than at any time since Priestly revised the prayer book and Jefferson abridged the New Testament. Indeed, even scientists who formally are agnostics seem to have a deeper appreciation of the ultimate majesty and mystery of the universe than do many conventional creedal Christians.

Surely in all of these developments we can discern the hand of the Holy Spirit, stirring up the church. But something must be said of the Spirit's long and patient work among those who have prepared the way—often without seeing any positive result, and sometimes facing what must have seemed to be utter defeat. Three vignettes must suffice.

(1) In the middle of the last century, a new liturgy book was prepared for use among German-speaking Calvinists located primarily in Pennsylvania and Ohio. In 1855 Charles Baird had published *Eutaxia* or *The Presbyterian Liturgies,* containing eucharistic liturgies written by Calvin, Knox, and others. It had shaken American Calvinists, who had wrongly assumed that

liturgical formulations were the antithesis of what their founders had advocated and intended. In the same era there developed at the German Reformed theological seminary in Mercersburg, Pennsylvania, a new study of liturgy promoted by two of the most prominent theologians of their time: John Williamson Nevin, a systematician, and Philip Schaff, a church historian.

Both men, together with a number of pastors in their area, diligently prepared a new liturgy for their denomination, restoring to prominence Calvin's own teaching about the Eucharist. After years of work had been put into it, the book was voted down, never to have official use. Its views of worship, particularly of the Lord's Supper, were too controversial. They took seriously the corporate nature of the church, which ran afoul of frontier individualism, and they set forth a sacramental communication of the gospel that was inimical to the prevailing revivalism of Charles G. Finney. Yet the fruits of this "Mercersburg Movement," as it came to be called, have had a great influence in our own time, for which its leaders could not have hoped on the day their new worship book was rejected by their small denomination of recent immigrants.

(2) Earlier in our own century in England, liturgical leaders of vision began to revise the *Book of Common Prayer*. Interrupted by World War I, the work dragged on and was not completed until 1928. By then it could not muster the necessary approval of Parliament, since political and religious currents had shifted during the book's long preparation. Parliament granted only that the book should be "deposited"—filed as a historical document without being given official status for the Church of England. Quite a defeat for those who had spent half a lifetime of labor in its production! Yet the "deposited Prayer Book" was consulted again and again by subsequent revisers of eucharistic liturgy across the world; in its exile, the book exerted enormous influence.

(3) There was born in Belgium in 1873 a man named Lambert Beauduin, who would become a monk of the Benedictine order. He thus was heir to intense, but virtually secret, liturgical labors by members of his order in the nineteenth century. These

monks, finding in monastic libraries books that had not been read in centuries, perceived that the worship of the Roman Catholic Church had gone awry and was in desperate need of reformation. These things they talked of furtively, in their inner circles, for fear of rejection by high church authorities.

Beauduin, at first a member of a prestigious theological faculty in Rome, soon became very controversial for his progressive opinions about ecumenism in general and liturgy in particular. In 1931 he was condemned for false teaching by a church tribunal in Rome and was sent off to virtual exile in a French abbey. The disastrous culmination of the effectiveness of a brilliant and prophetic man? Not quite.

In France, Beauduin met and deeply influenced an Italian priest who had been named Papal Nuncio to Paris at the close of World War II. The monk convinced the bureaucrat that the Roman Catholic Church needed to be turned upside down and shaken thoroughly, particularly in its worship and its relation to other Christian bodies. Beauduin did not live quite long enough to see his condemned views totally vindicated, but before he died in 1960 he saw former Nuncio Angelo Guiseppe Cardinal Roncalli elected to the papacy. The world knows this courageous renovator of the church as Pope John XXIII, who convened the Second Vatican Council and put at the top of its agenda the reformation of the sacred liturgy.

Can the faithful working of the Spirit in these three instances—and thousands more—be denied? Surely not. And from such evident divine persistence and fidelity in the face of human resistance and weakness, we find strength to forge ahead in our own time.

## CHAPTER FIVE

# TOWARD A RENEWAL OF EUCHARISTIC UNDERSTANDING

Attempts through the centuries to understand, or at least to characterize, the Eucharist and to practice it with integrity confirm that it is a subject on which the church is not content to be silent; when silence has prevailed, distortions have stepped in with destructive power. And while mystery is a necessary component of eucharistic faith, we cannot simply retreat into mystery without also falling into danger. Therefore, we now address two crucial questions: In the light of all we have seen thus far, what should characterize eucharistic theology for today? How can a renewed theology be effectively transmitted to congregations?

In answer to the first question, we will gather together the strands we have discussed earlier and suggest components of the contemporary enterprise. The hallmarks set forth here are not restricted to one particular theological system, for that would have too limited an appeal and too transitory a life. Instead areas are suggested for investigation and elaboration by those who construct contemporary theologies from various perspectives, and particularly by the "consumers" who select from among the various theological and ecumenical options. These components should characterize good liturgies as well as theological constructions more generally, for liturgical texts embody and convey theology to local congregations in ways not always recognized.

We turn now to the components of contemporary eucharistic theology themselves, and thereafter to ways these can be incorporated into eucharistic reorientation through teaching and preaching.

## COMPONENTS OF A RENEWED EUCHARISTIC THEOLOGY

*1. The Eucharist is to be seen above all as sacrament—God's gift to us.* As we have seen in the biblical story, God at all points takes the initiative: creating our world, making covenant, becoming incarnate in Jesus, establishing the church as a community of faith and witness, and inaugurating a kingdom that will have no end. Of all of these, we human beings are recipients at the hand of a gracious God.

The Eucharist should set forth before us this God who goes out ahead of us. No matter how much we may initially see our participation in the feast as a seeking after God, ultimately we come to confess that even our seeking is but the result of a yearning God has put within us and that it is God who first seeks us.

Diatribes against sacraments by members of the left-wing of the Reformation (in favor of seeing the Supper as an ordinance only) grew out of justified complaints against medieval tendencies to quantify grace and transmit it mechanically. But the historical situation is very different now, and sacramental language and practice no longer carry the unfortunate baggage they brought with them in the sixteenth century.

Indeed we may now be nearly 180 degrees away from the Reformation situation; medieval life was pervaded by an awareness of the presence of God, and theologians needed to guard against tendencies to take for granted the ready availability of God's aid. But in an increasingly secularized culture, God has been forced to the margins of life. The present danger is less that we will suppose we can constantly manipulate God than that we will regard God as impersonal, distant, and One accessible to us primarily *in extremis,* with prayer being seen largely as a last-minute appeal in the face of threatening tragedies. The Eucharist as sacrament, by contrast, shows forth the One who feeds us daily and enters into the feasting with us in order that we may thereby recognize how fully divine love pervades the whole of creation.

Some understandings of the Eucharist have been what technically are called "irruptionist"—a God outside of ordinary life at times breaks in upon that life. If these understandings served a good purpose in the past, they are increasingly detrimental to a world that already has pushed God to its edges.

For our day, a more useful metaphor of God's manner of working may be found in tapestry. The colors of various threads are visible to the viewer only in particular places, as determined by the weaver. That is not because these colors suddenly drop in upon the fabric from the outside but because at many points they exist on the underside, unseen by the viewer. Always they are present, but sometimes hidden and sometimes manifest. Likewise, God is not an outsider who periodically pops in (and then out) of life. God is with us always. Divine work we can see assures us of divine work we cannot see. The God who labors incognito in our midst provides the sacraments, lest we mistake invisibility for inactivity or absence.

*2. A necessary corollary is that the Eucharist is a reliable means of grace, yet is not grace itself.* For Christians, grace resides in God's action in Jesus Christ, who is the clearest manifestation of God among us. Although not the only manifestation, God-in-Christ is our primary clue to discovering God in the world around us. The Eucharist, our *anamnesis* of Christ, thus puts us in touch with aspects of God's presence that we might not otherwise see so clearly. Therefore the Eucharist is a means of grace—one of various divinely given ways in which we experience Christ in our midst.

Among some Protestants there is a fear that such talk implies a kind of automatic and irresistible dispensation of grace. But consider preaching as a corollary. These same Protestants would strongly affirm that faith in Christ can come by preaching, as set forth in Romans 10:14-17; nor would they take umbrage at anyone who said, "I found Christ through the preaching of Rev. So-and-So." This would not be taken to suggest that the sermon of that preacher produced an automatic conveying of grace or that everyone within the sound of the preacher's voice must have been affected equally. Nor would the differing affects and our human ability to resist them be taken as a denial of the effective power of preaching. To say that the sacrament is a means of grace is to affirm that it can indeed effectively bring Christ into our experience, but not as if by magic or such that all communicants will be given a grace they cannot reject. The sacrament creates the condition for our renewal as we enter ever more fully into the covenant initiated for us and with us by the One who hosts the feast.

*3. The Christ who is proclaimed through the Eucharist is the whole Christ, and the proclamation should embody the full saving work of the feast's Host.*[1] We are thus reminded of the incarnation. Just as once God came to us in the humble form of a baby, so also God comes to us in the ordinary things of bread and wine. The many meals in which Jesus engaged and the use of meals he made in the parables tie the Eucharist to the Savior's entire ministry of teaching and healing. The breaking of bread and the pouring of wine powerfully recall Jesus' body rent upon the cross and his blood spilled out upon the ground. And our eucharistic feasts both recall Christ's resurrection (when those who believed ate with their risen Lord) and Messiah's final reign in glory (when all shall feast at the heavenly banquet).

Not all of these meanings can be equally evident in every eucharistic celebration. Where the liturgical calendar is followed, the various festivals of the church's year will naturally highlight the meaning particularly appropriate to that day. But over time, all of Christ's work should be evident.

We have seen in chapter 4 that because of certain historical conditions the medieval Mass came to concentrate so completely on Calvary that almost all other meanings were obscured. Due to its anxiety about purgatory, the church became preoccupied with the Mass as a propitiatory sacrifice. The unfortunate result was a concentration in the Eucharist on the Lord's atoning work to the exclusion of almost everything else.

In some ways the Reformation only made matters worse. In the propitiatory Mass there was at least some sense of an objective action occurring; when Protestants understandably tossed out the idea of sacramental propitiation, often what was left was simply a reverent but very subjective contemplation of the events that historically surrounded Calvary. Added to that was a complicating factor: The Reformers abolished penance as a sacrament, yet insisted upon confession of sin. Thus the Eucharist came to bear the weight of a penitential rite, through which the theme of human unworthiness came to run like an *idée fixe* in music.

Until recently, therefore, in virtually all Protestant churches, the sacrament had strong elements of subjective Good Friday devotions with an overlay of individualistic penitence. Now we have become greatly aware of the problem and have sought to alleviate it by stressing that the Eucharist is a resurrection meal. Indeed it is, but the tide threatens to turn too strongly in the other direction. Wanting to escape the morbidity and subjectiveness of the "perpetual Good Friday" mentality, eucharistic celebration has sometimes become as irrepressibly happy and exuberant as its antecedent was sorrowful and introspective.

At its best, this kind of eucharistic observance centers on the resurrection and reign of God to the exclusion of all else. Certainly the Eucharist is both the memory of Emmaus made present to us (*anamnesis*) and the foretaste of the Great Supper in heaven, already with us through hope (*prolepsis*). But what of Jesus' humiliating birth and multi-faceted ministry of compassion and instruction about the demands of discipleship? And how can we get to the empty tomb, let alone to the eternal habitation, except by way of the cross?

At its worst, a triumphalistic type of Eucharist centers simply on what is called rather vaguely "the celebration of life." Never mind that the philosopher Thomas Hobbes asserted with some cogency that human life is "solitary, poor, nasty, brutish, and short"—or that many people arrive at the Eucharist hurting deeply from difficulties in their personal lives or sorely concerned about the sufferings of others in the world around them. Surely these persons need and want the Good News; if they are given instead a chirpy optimism (which suggests they have no reason to be distressed and perhaps should feel guilty about their anxiety or "lack of faith"), they rightly sense that they are being both mocked and cheated. Not only has everything of the Jesus story before the resurrection been by-passed, but they have been shown an empty cheeriness rather than the empty tomb.

The tendencies just noted usually do not exist in denominationally approved eucharistic prayers; they are more characteristic of ad hoc prayers and other elements in the surrounding liturgy—particularly in the sermon. But such surrounding elements can readily shout down even the most carefully prepared Prayer of Great Thanksgiving.

Balance is difficult to obtain, and overreaction to previous situations ever threatens to create one imbalance to replace another. Contemporary eucharistic theology should seek to set forth the full range of the church's experiences of and affirmations about Jesus Christ: humble incarnation, ministry of teaching and healing, sacrificial death, transforming resurrection, presence in the church and world, and ultimate reign of righteousness.

Finally, the legitimate motif of resurrection needs to be carefully investigated and interpreted today lest we settle for an understanding that is too meager and too readily rejected or too easily and glibly appropriated by contemporary thinkers. Popular piety tends to settle for the resuscitation of the corpse of Jesus and supposes that anything else is somehow a "denial" of the resurrection. In fact, at least certain varieties of "anything else" see the resurrection to be something much more than resuscitation. These understand Jesus not simply to have returned to a prolonged form of the same kind of existence he had before the crucifixion but to have entered into an entirely new mode of existence.

That newness breaks out of our usual categories and ushers us into an eternity that is far more than an infinite expanse of time. Just as true peace is more than the absence of war, so also true resurrection is more than the absence of death. Nor does this understanding of resurrection as something more than resuscitation necessarily imply that nothing "happened" to the physical body of Jesus, so that his bones may yet be discovered somewhere; what happened involved total transformation, not simply the reversal of the biological process called death.

Is it not possible that the sacrament signals to us this very kind of transformation—and even participates in it, as the risen One is made known in the breaking of the bread? Indeed, it was perhaps this very transformation that the medieval theologians were groping to describe in their sometimes tortured theological controversies. The fact that we can no longer accept their labored explanations (and perhaps can never find any adequate explanation of our own) does not mean that we should surrender crucial affirmations about the utterly transformative power of the resurrection communicated to us through bread and wine.

*4. Inseparable from all of this, and often also obscured, is the work of the Holy Spirit.* In contrast to the impoverished understanding in the West of the Spirit's work in the Eucharist, the Eastern Orthodox churches have maintained a rich heritage from which we can benefit in meaning, if not in form.[2]

Certainly universal Christian teaching affirms the activity of the Spirit throughout the life of the church. But the Spirit has a particular role in eucharistic *anamnesis.* Before going to the cross, Jesus tells the disciples, "The Holy Spirit . . . will teach you everything, and remind you of all that I have said to you" (John 14:26). This function of "reminding" is closely akin to *anamnesis* and has sometimes given the Spirit the title of "The Remembrancer." Hence, what we specifically "do in remembrance" of Jesus is done through the agency of the Holy Spirit. It is by the power of the Spirit that bread and wine can mean more than gustatory pleasure and physiological nutrition, that these ordinary table items can be the body and blood of Christ—Christ incarnate, crucified, risen, present in the world, and reigning in righteousness.

In a more general way also, the Spirit is the One who brings the risen Lord into the present experience of the church. Indeed, some theologians would argue that the Spirit is the presence of the risen One within the believing community. Hence the Spirit's work in the Eucharist is part and parcel of the Spirit's wider ministry of transformation. The Holy Spirit who can make bread and wine mean more than we can imagine bread and wine to be acts similarly in our lives and in the life of the whole creation.

Frequently, Christians have stumbled over the use of physical things to declare the goodness of God. Thus often it is suggested that we need to free ourselves of physical concerns to be more spiritual. Some even suggest that sacraments are "crutches for the weak of faith," and that when spiritual maturity is attained these supports are no longer required; thus one "grows out of" a need for the Eucharist. But is it, in fact, the other way around—that the Holy Spirit infuses the things of creation with such deep meaning that growing in grace binds us more closely to sacramental activity?

It is an observable fact that human beings crave visible tokens of love. Two individuals covenanting in marriage are rarely content with spoken vows or even with a certificate of matrimony in witness thereof. So rings or other objects are given and received as signs of mutual promises. Two nations ending hostilities are not satisfied with verbal agreements, nor even with written treaty documents. They exchange the very pens with which the papers are signed and, likely, put them on display in national museums.

Similarly, many of us have drawers, closets, and attics full of mementos of one relationship or another. We would not think of throwing out these photographs, clippings, invitations, place cards, dried flowers, or old letters. Ultimately the persons attorneys call our "heirs and assigns" will have to toss them; as they do, likely they will mutter, "Why on earth wasn't that gotten rid of years ago?" The answer lies in an innate need for outward and visible signs of an inward, intangible reality—a need God understands because it is a part of our created nature, and therefore a need to which God ministers by the working of the Holy Spirit in the material things of sacraments.

At first it may seem odd to assert that the Spirit can give things meaning that they do not have on their own, and thus can make ordinary objects signs of divine love and power. But the oddity evaporates when we confront the importance of signs and how they function even in nonreligious settings. For example, a party dress or a parka in a store window means only that people deem differing kinds of attire appropriate for particular occasions. But when bereaved parents refuse to give up the favorite party dress or parka of their deceased child, it is because the garments have been infused with a different meaning: They have come to be "signs" of a treasured relationship, not just ways of covering the body according to accepted social conventions.[3]

"Advanced" cultures tend to explain this in "pop psychology" terms that make the phenomenon easily dismissed. The parents have inappropriately transferred to an object an emotional attachment previously related to a person, thus making a fetish of that object. While such transference can be neurotic, we must ask whether it is necessarily so. May it be that "primitive" cultures have a deeper psychological understanding in seeing "spirit" and "physical" to be so intertwined that the dress or parka has become "invested" with the very being of the one who once wore it (the "mana," in anthropological terminology). (*Invest* is not originally a financial term but one having to do with attire; hence our words *vest, vestment,* and *vesture.*) The garment worn by the person who is no longer observably present has thereby become a "sign" of that person and cannot be readily dismissed as mere clothing. The garment bears within it something of the reality of the relationship, as recognized by serious psychologists (as distinguished from the "pop" variety).

Since all of this is a part of our human condition, is it so odd that the Holy Spirit should invest bread and wine with new meaning—so that they become signs of a deep covenantal relationship with God, "signs of grace"? Most important, these go beyond what is signified by the party dress or the parka, for unlike the deceased child, Christ is risen and in our midst. Therefore, the Spirit causes bread and wine to be signs invested with this living Presence.

Careful work at the intersection of pneumatology, psychology, and anthropology may enable us to appreciate the words "This is my body" in a way that they have not been appreciated since Nominalism precipitated the collapse of both Extreme and Moderate Realism.

Recent eucharistic prayers, both Catholic and Protestant, have taken care to restore a specific invocation of the Holy Spirit (technically called the *epiklesis,* from Greek terms meaning "to call upon"). In one way or another, these petitions (preserved in the East and long absent in the West) ask God to send the Spirit upon the bread and wine that they may be for us the body and blood of Christ. Often the invocation continues, appropriately asking that the Spirit will also come upon the congregation present, that the church may truly be the body of Christ in the world. This leads directly to the next necessary component in contemporary eucharistic theology.

5. *Because the Eucharist is a meal of the church, imbedded in any theology of the sacrament is an ecclesiology—assumptions about the nature of the church.* But is this ecclesiology the one we wish to advance? That question is crucial because usually the assumptions about the church are concealed—and therefore unexamined. But like subliminal messages on television, implied ecclesiology exercises its teaching function in the midst of the congregation even when it is unnoticed.

To be concrete, if a liturgy speaks primarily about the eucharistic benefits that accrue to me, abounding in the pronouns *I, me,* and *my,* then the church will be viewed as a collection of rather disconnected individuals, each of whom participates because of what he or she can receive in return. Attendance at worship in a church so conceived is optional. I attend when I need something because I have had a difficult week; on other Sundays I may well find "better" things to do. And how I use my time, money, and talent between Sundays is a matter solely between me and God. This is an individualistic and self-serving ecclesiology—but one that will not be strange to most readers.[4]

On the other hand, suppose a eucharistic liturgy talks about the church as a grateful community of the resurrection into which we have been called by Christ in order that the world may come to believe through our testimony. Suppose that the prayers use primarily plural pronouns: *we* and *us* (as ministers of Christ) and *they* and *them* (those to whom we are sent as witnesses). Then church participation is not really optional unless (a) I am not sufficiently aware of God's goodness to give thanks; (b) I have little regard for Sunday as a perpetual commemoration of the resurrection; and (c) I care so little about Christ's call and the welfare of the world that it matters not whether I am a good

witness or an indifferent one. Furthermore, what I do with my time, money, and talent may call for the mutual wisdom of the community of fellow Christians, and certainly implies accountability both to them and to the world apart from the church, as well as to God. Such an ecclesiology is corporate and dwells more on what we share with others and receive together than on what I as an individual get out of my practice of religion.

The point is that not only should we pick our ecclesiology carefully, but more important is the fact that the Eucharist by its very nature makes certain kinds of ecclesiology defensible and others questionable—if only we stop to think about what we are doing. In the best sense of the term, the Eucharist itself "imposes" an identification upon the church, for the Eucharist is not only a meal of the church, but also is one through which the church is constituted and empowered. It is not accidental that the phrase "body of Christ" refers both to the Eucharist and to the church.

Congregations typically do a lot of eating and drinking together—church dinners, coffee hours, receptions, and refreshments at all sorts of gatherings. These are important, but should be seen as subsidiary to and different from the Holy Meal. It is in the Eucharist that Christians most clearly meet their Lord and join together in spiritual union while eating and drinking together.

All of the other kinds of eating can also take place at the Rotary Club, PTA functions, garden club meetings, gatherings sponsored by one or another political party, and social functions generally. The Eucharist, by contrast, is unique to the church. No one else has it, or should be expected to know what to do with it. It is, in fact, a part of the "strangeness" of the church.

That is why the church asserts that the Eucharist is "for the baptized." This restriction is not meant to be elitist, nor is it a matter of inhospitality or bad manners. It is meant as an affirmation that Christian discipleship presumes an identity given by God and a commitment accepted by us in the church's regular initiation rites; further, the Eucharist is a means of grace given by the power of the Holy Spirit to those who continue in that discipleship, that their faith may increase as they experience their risen Lord, and that they may be equipped for the forms of ministry committed to them. The Eucharist is unlike the congregational social hour, to which everyone may indeed be invited. Rather, sharing in the sacrament is one of the marks of being the church.

A strong ecclesiology is necessary to prevent the Eucharist from being a privatistic exercise of spiritual interaction between God and believers singly, on the one hand, and from degenerating into "refreshments in church" on the other. The former problem has been pervasive among both Catholics and Protestants until recently. Now, having been challenged in many quarters, the individualistic bent threatens to give way to a well-meaning inclusivism that sees no reason whatsoever for differentiating between who is invited to the Lord's Table and who is invited to the coffee hour. Only a renewed understanding of what it means to be the church will rescue us from the twin dangers of this Scylla and Charybdis. Such an understanding can, however, draw on the positive aspects of each side of the problem.

On the one side, those who see the Eucharist only as a one-to-one encounter with God do not perceive that the sacrament is relational. What needs to be added to their understanding is that it creates relationships among all those at the table as well as between each communicant and God. Those who are drawn to God are also drawn together around the banquet. Further, the sharing and interaction experienced at the table is the model and motivation for the church's mission in the world.

On the other side, those who see the Eucharist as a feast that should embrace the multitudes grasp the fact that God's love is offered to all and is not reserved for a coterie of the devout. What needs to be added to their understanding is the fact that the church is charged by God with the task not simply of bringing ever larger numbers of people into the church building but of challenging those who do come to be committed and informed disciples; only in this way will the congregation truly function as Christ's living body in the world instead of being just an assembly of persons who, for a variety of reasons, find religious interaction helpful.

Also closely related to any ecclesiology connected with the Eucharist is the matter of inter-communion between Christians of different denominational bodies. Attached to that is the whole issue of ordination in relation to presiding at or distributing the sacrament. These matters will be addressed in chapter 7.

On the issues of ecclesiology, enormous work remains to be done—likely more than on any other issue discussed in this chapter. In contrast to the private Mass of the solitary priest, the Reformers insisted, "No communion without a congregation." At a legal level they won, but at a practical level they lost. Too often communicants, even when totally surrounded by fellow believers, view the moment of reception, in particular, as "my private time with God." Complained one Methodist when the Wesleyan practice of singing hymns during the distribution was being reinstated: "How dare the congregation sing while I am trying to commune with my God at the altar."

Through the Eucharist, God struggles to teach us about community in its broadest reaches—the community of humanity, indeed the community of the cosmos. But this divine word to us will not be clearly heard until the church recovers the deep conviction that it is not an assortment of individuals at prayer in the same space, but rather is itself a community of prayer, at times gathered in one place but more usually scattered abroad in daily life like a bit of yeast that leavens the whole lump of dough.

6. *Just as there is always an ecclesiology, recognized or not, so also always there is an eschatology—some assumptions about the goal and final outcome of things in the providence of God.* Covert eschatologies may be very anemic ("Not much will ever change, actually") or excessively idealistic ("All we need to do is have faith, and everything will turn out wonderfully well"). But neither undue pessimism nor a trust in automatic progress humanly achieved characterizes sound Christian eschatology. Furthermore, much popular eschatology is escapist ("All will be well in heaven when we die. No sooner, no later. So let's ignore present problems and focus on the future.")

In contrast, eschatology most defensible for our time believes that the future as envisioned should have an impact on the present, albeit imperfectly so. Thus future hope and present action are intertwined. This prevents twin distortions: (1) the notion that God will do everything at the end of time, which leads to an acceptance of the status quo in the present and makes human action unnecessary: "There will be in heaven a great banquet at which all may join, being equal in status; until then we simply have to put up with whatever injustices life visits upon us"; (2) the notion that we must (and can) do everything on our own now, which leads in many cases to discouragement and even disillusionment when earthly perfection is not reached: "We must achieve total justice on earth now without making excuses or supposing that we are going to get any supernatural help or waiting for some great feast of joy in the hereafter. Granted, we may wear ourselves out in the process."

In the kind of eschatology proposed here, the future is seen as a reality that tugs on us in the present. Concerning our regular Eucharists: "Feast after feast thus comes and passes by; yet, passing, points to the glad feast of above."[5] Further, the "table etiquette" of that glad feast above is to be put into effect in our present world, to the best of our capacities as given and sustained by God. Thus there is indeed something for us to do here and now other than to wait for heaven to appear. But we do not write the rules, nor do we naively expect that society at large will embrace willingly and totally even our best efforts at reform.

The church is engaged in perpetual struggle; final triumph is the purview of God. However, far from being left to wonder, agnostic-like, as to whether God will ever act, in the resurrection and our share in its benefits we have God's assurance that the final kingdom has been already inaugurated, though not yet fully consummated. The victim of Calvary is the victor for eternity. The Christ made known to us in the breaking of the bread at the Eucharist is the same Host who will preside at the Great Feast of the Lamb.

To this Great Feast, guests will come from north and south and east and west to sit at table. We who now share the Eucharist are joined in unity with those who preceded us, even as we struggle to open our earthly tables to all of God's people, even as we seek to make the present creation conform to the image of the new heaven and the new earth envisioned in the Revelation. But as the Revelator warns us, the route to the heavenly city is a rough one. The Eucharist provides strength for the journey and consolation when cares overtake us.

Indeed, it is thus that we are united with Christ, who also struggled mightily en route to the cross. Our attempts to be faithful to the heavenly vision (no matter how incomplete the result) constitute our sacrifice of praise and thanksgiving, which mysteriously is joined with Christ's sacrificial self-offering at Calvary. The Eucharist as sacrifice is an idea not to be spurned simply because it was misused in the Middle Ages. But it is best understood eschatologically: The Lamb upon the eucharistic altar is the Lamb who sits upon the throne. That Lamb is alone worthy

> "to receive power and wealth and
> wisdom and might
> and honor and glory and
> blessing!"
>
> (Rev. 5:12)

All of the living sacrifice of ourselves that we on earth can muster ascends to that Lamb like a fragrant offering.

Thus the future tugs at us and motivates us. At the same time it frustrates us because we can neither evade the present by fleeing into the future nor reform the present to be the perfection that we believe will characterize God's eternal reign. With such an ambiguous reality the church must wrestle continually, like Jacob at the Jabbock, until day breaks, content meanwhile only to know that God blesses us in our blessing of the bread and wine.

## EUCHARISTIC REORIENTATION THROUGH TEACHING AND PREACHING

Much of that endless wrestling will take the form of teaching and preaching in the congregation in order that new understandings of the Eucharist may be grasped and new practices put into effect.

Because what follows is closely related to parish programs of education and preaching, some traditional strategies should be challenged. Clergy and other Christian educators too often use an approach of "all eggs in one basket." For example, suppose it is deemed wise to reform a congregation's eucharistic understanding and practice through a program of adult education. A typical approach is to schedule and announce a four- or six-week study for interested persons, with each session lasting sixty to ninety minutes. As well intended as this may be, it has drawbacks. At best only a remnant of the Sunday morning congregation will return for a Sunday or Wednesday evening study series. Knowing this, pastors may say, "Well, instead of that, I will preach about the sacrament so that everyone who attends Sunday worship can benefit."

Both approaches put inordinate trust in concentrated presentations. These will not be without an effect, but greater effectiveness may be achieved through a more diffuse and extended approach. Instead of one sermon about the Eucharist now and again, it is wiser to make brief references to the Eucharist in sermons on a variety of subjects. When preaching on stewardship, mention may be made of the example of sharing set forth for us at the Lord's Table. A sermon on the nature of the church can take note of the fact that in the Eucharist the church engages in a unique occasion of fellowship among its members in the presence of God—a fellowship that should characterize the congregation in all phases of its life together. A sermon about prayer can note that prayer is not simply asking for things, but is praising God—as we do each time we offer the eucharistic prayer. A sermon on the incarnation may note the way One who at Bethlehem came to us in human flesh and blood now comes to us in a similarly humble manner in bread and wine. And so on for other themes.

Because the sacrament reveals the Christ who is Lord of all aspects of the church's life, there can hardly be a sermon subject to which the sacrament is not closely connected. The identification of these connections need not—probably should not—be lengthy. More is achieved though brief comments again and again than through one or two sermons entirely on the subject—though the latter can be both necessary and appropriate.

However, where attendance declines on communion Sunday, it is the better part of wisdom to preach about the Eucharist on other Sundays. We cannot change the minds of those who are not present. Similarly, those who feel disinclined to receive the sacrament are not likely to attend a series of adult education classes on the meaning of the Eucharist. It is more helpful to infuse other kinds of educational sessions with insights into the relationship between the subject of discussion and eucharistic experience.

Further, eucharistic reform should be promoted in other ways and at all age levels. It should be built into church school curricula for children and youth and incorporated into retreat and camping experiences, and into the programs of a full range of church activities. (This is not to suggest that the sacrament be observed in these settings; the Eucharist is primarily an experience for the entire congregation on Sunday, not the preserve of sub-groups. But learning and reflection on the meaning of the sacrament can occur in each of these situations.) Media of every appropriate sort may be pressed into service, from church newsletters to videotapes and other forms of visual presentation.

Finally, even where one or more sermons, study sessions, and other experiences are devoted explicitly to the Eucharist, only a novice would attempt to cram in everything outlined above. Selectivity and common sense are in order; particularly in the instance of discussions and other verbal presentations, there is great wisdom in the homespun adage that "the mind can absorb only as much as the seat can endure."

Plans for reorienting eucharistic piety in a congregation should be made with deliberation and great care. Never should a teaching or practice be snatched from people (who probably have been very well educated into it, even if for bad reasons) without in return giving something of a least equal value.

The easiest reforms to effect are those that are supported by similar reforms in other constituencies. Congregations as well as individuals fear, above all else, being judged "odd." Hence they will respond more readily to teachings and practices they discover to be taking hold in other parishes with which they are in communication. After visiting another congregation or talking to its members, people often return to their own parishes and say with great relief, "They do it that way, too. We aren't the only ones." Clergy and other leaders of reform do well, therefore, to consult with one another and engage in efforts that are mutually reinforcing.

Both skill and patience will be required to effect reform. The difficulties we have inherited have, for the most part, endured for centuries, or even a millennium. They will not be altered quickly or easily; still, the benefits to be achieved through a renewed understanding of the Eucharist are both highly desirable and attainable.

## CHAPTER SIX

# CONDUCTING THE EUCHARIST

The way in which the Eucharist is observed in the congregation will both reflect and effect a renewed understanding of the sacrament. If a new eucharistic understanding is forged and taught but the Eucharist is still observed as it was fifty years ago, teaching and practice will contradict each other in detrimental ways. On the other hand, reform in the way the service is conducted can create what educators call "a teachable moment" as the congregation seeks to understand why the rite is being conducted differently. It is a combination of communicating a new understanding of the sacrament and of conducting the service in a new manner that will most effectively bring about significant changes in eucharistic attitude and appreciation.

Hence we now consider the very practical matters of eucharistic celebration, under the categories of context, rite, actions, elements, furnishings, and people.

### CONTEXT

The context of the Eucharist is normally the Sunday service of the local congregation. *Norm* here does not mean "the only possibility" but the practice that governs other possibilities. That is, the Eucharist can justifiably be celebrated on a weekday at a wedding or funeral, in a church conference or retreat setting, or in a hospital room or residence. But what is done in these alternate circumstances is derived from the congregational service for the Lord's Day. The usual practices may be altered to meet circumstances (such that an abbreviated form of prayer is used in an intensive care unit or the manner of distribution is altered as dictated by the setting in a retreat center), but the Eucharist is not invented *de novo* for each of these occasions.

Nor do certain circumstances apart from the Sunday service set the policy for all else. It is justifiable for the Eucharist to be celebrated in a residence because one of the family members is house-bound, but this is not to be taken to mean that every family unit in the parish should expect to have communion brought to the home. The gathered congregation is the place of communion for all who are able to attend.

The Sunday service will have a double focus: (1) the reading and exposition of the scriptures in the context of prayer and praise and (2) the sacrament. Particularly in cases where the sacramental observance has been very infrequent (two to four times a year), often the sermon has suffered on communion Sunday, being greatly reduced in length or even jettisoned entirely.[1] Ironically, the time "saved" was often consumed by long-winded announcements or verbose "table dismissals."[2]

As the frequency of the Eucharist increases, and as it more and more comes to be associated with the principal days of the liturgical calendar, the abolition or severe reduction of the sermon becomes totally untenable. First, the WASPish assumption that worship can take only fifty-nine minutes and fifty-nine seconds needs to be challenged. Second, where the church parking lot absolutely must be emptied of traffic after the 9:30 service to make room for the 11:00 worshipers, the service should be examined to see how else time can be saved. For example, the anthem can be sung while the offering is being received, and hymns may be sung during the distribution (particularly in churches where communicants move from their seats to serving stations), rather than being used as separate items in the service. It may be possible to omit the creed.[3] Often the mechanics of the distribution can be streamlined without sacrificing a sense of reverence.

While the controlling nature of the Sunday service allows for adaptations in other settings, it also proscribes certain kinds of adaptations, most notably the "silent come-and-go" communions that have become widespread in some places for special weekdays. Thus it is announced in a church newsletter, for example:

> On Ash Wednesday, the chapel will be open from 6:00 A.M. to 9:00 P.M., with communion elements available to you throughout the time. Come whenever convenient, and remain as long as you wish. At the point in your personal meditation that you feel it appropriate, receive a portion of the bread and wine. Please maintain silence throughout, so as not to disturb others who may be present at the same time.

Note what is not done: There is no congregational interaction, nor any action of the clergy, no scripture or sermon, no offertory action, no corporate prayer of Great Thanksgiving (even if prayer sheets are available for private use), and no distribution. Can we dare to say we are doing what Jesus did? Judged by the Sunday service, this permutation is weighed in the balance and found wanting. Its model is not the Christian congregation at prayer but the convenience store. This kind of service is most easily recognized as an unwarranted distortion by asking those among whom it is popular how they would react to receiving the following letter:

> Dear family members:
>
> As you know, for many years we have hosted our family's Christmas dinner. This year we have decided to do it differently. We will not, in fact, be at home on December 25. But the house will be unlocked all day, with food out on the table. Come whenever you wish. Stay as long as you like. But please, while there, do not talk to anyone else, lest they should be concentrating about something else. And a Merry Christmas, every one!

Note also the covert ecclesiology in the silent come-and-go observance. Far from being a community nurtured by scripture and its exposition (while joining in prayer and praise) and by the sacrament, the church is seen to be a collection of individuals who engage in independent devotional acts. Either this church does not need clergy (since clergy need not be present at this preeminent form of worship), or those clergy have transformative powers. Before anyone arrives they do something special to the bread and wine and then they depart, though the effect of what they do lingers, apparently within the bread and wine themselves. Surely no church can claim integrity to the New Testament vision of Christian community with an ecclesiology so weak, individualistic, and possibly magical.

Sound ecclesiology also dictates another aspect of eucharistic practice. If a congregation holds more than one service on Sunday morning, the Eucharist should be celebrated at all services or at least at the principal service. The tactic of trying to ease a congregation gently into a weekly Eucharist by scheduling this for a few interested people at an early hour, followed by a principal service without Eucharist, is at best a temporary expedient—and it all too readily backfires. It can create, in effect, two dissonant congregations using one building—with the earlier group being viewed either as the superpious or the slightly strange. Lurking behind this is also an ecclesiology that is highly suspect.

## THE RITE

By *rite* we mean here the text employed when conducting the Eucharist. Usually rites are denominationally determined, and while once that created noticeable disparities from one denomination to another, today the differences are greatly minimized. Recent revisions in any of the major denominations have much in common, owing to a mutual dependence on the ancient tradition of the church rather than on variations that arose at the Reformation and later. Indeed, Roman Catholic rites and those of many Protestant denominations are virtually indistinguishable these days, not the least because all recent revisers have looked over their shoulders at the work of Hippolytus more so than that of the Council of Trent or Luther and Calvin.

Despite all the jokes about a camel being a horse put together by a committee, denominational rites are more to be trusted than the work of individual writers; the latter can be idiosyncratic at best, and at worst ill-informed as to appropriate shape and content.

Those who work in denominations that expect the rites to be determined locally on a service-by-service basis are well advised to have as handy reference works the liturgy books of the major denominations that do provide carefully considered and well-written rites. These official rites may need adaptation to be suitable for other denominations, but (as every author knows) when starting to write, anything is better than a blank sheet of paper.

Most denominations no longer provide just one eucharistic rite, but several choices. Thus those who plan the service can select between the language of "thee" and "thou" and the more familiar speech of contemporary daily conversation. But often also separate rites are provided for non-festival Sundays, for festival occasions (Christmas Day, Epiphany, Holy Thursday, Easter Day, Day of Pentecost, and the like), and for the pastoral services including weddings and funerals.

The central prayer of the eucharistic rite is known by several names. In older rites it is called the Anaphora in Eastern Orthodoxy, the Canon of the Mass in Roman Catholicism, and the Prayer of Consecration or Communion Prayer among Protestants. In keeping with the recovery of the ancient term *eucharist* as the most suitable name for the sacrament, increasingly popular are the titles Great Thanksgiving, Great Prayer, Prayer of Thanksgiving, or simply Eucharistic Prayer.

Such prayers commonly have a particular form and content, as follows:

- An *Opening Dialogue* between celebrant and congregation, typically an updated version of Hippolytus's rite:

  The Lord be with you.
  
  And also with you.
  
  Lift up your hearts.
  
  We lift them to the Lord.
  
  Let us give thanks to the Lord our God.
  
  It is right to give our thanks and praise.
  
  It is always and in all places right to give thanks. . . .

- One or more *Prefaces* follow, perhaps preceded by a recounting of God's work throughout sacred history, especially that work prior to the coming of Christ. First there may be a "proper preface," which relates to a theme of a specific occasion. The proper preface for Christmas, for example, may read: "Because you gave your Son to be born among us, as one of us, that we might be redeemed from sin and receive adoption as your daughters and sons." Then follows the "general preface," which can be used on any occasion; for instance: "Therefore with angels and archangels and all the company of heaven, we praise your name, joining in their unending hymn."

- Then the congregation joins in singing or saying the *Sanctus* ("Holy"), based on Isaiah 6:3, and the *Benedictus qui venit* ("Blessed is he who comes"), based on Psalm 118:26 as quoted in Matthew 21:9 and parallels:

Holy, holy, holy Lord, God of power and might,
heaven and earth are full of your glory.
Hosanna in the highest.
Blessed is he who comes in the name of the Lord.
Hosanna in the highest.[4]

Then, if not recounted earlier, God's acts in history may be proclaimed here, including the work of Christ prior to his final journey to Jerusalem.

The next three components may occur in differing orders.

- The *Institution Narrative,* whether from 1 Corinthians 11:23-25 or one of the Gospels, is recited either here or (in some traditions) at another prominent place.
- An *Anamnesis* of the fuller work of Christ's self-offering is included, setting the passion in the larger context of resurrection and reign.
- The *Epiklesis* calls upon God to send the Holy Spirit upon the bread and wine and, in many cases, upon the congregation, that God's people may rightly offer their sacrifice of praise and service.

The Eucharistic Prayer then often includes:

- *Intercessions* for the living and dead, or a commemoration of the saints who have preceded us and join with us.
- *Petitions* for the unity of Christ's holy church and the manifestation of Christ's eternal kingdom.

Finally, the Prayer concludes with:

- A spoken *Doxology,* Trinitarian in form.
- An *Amen* sung or spoken by the congregation.

Usually the Lord's Prayer is prayed in unison immediately thereafter.

Despite the appearance of complexity to what is outlined above, a well-written eucharistic prayer can be remarkably concise and can be spoken without undue haste in three minutes—about the time required to sing "A Mighty Fortress Is Our God," or "How Great Thou Art," and considerably less time than is consumed by many extemporaneous eucharistic prayers.

In addition to the eucharistic prayer, most rites also supply subsidiary prayers, such as a prayer when the bread and wine are received at the Lord's Table (or uncovered if already in place), and closing prayers after the reception of communion. Some rites provide resources for the day's service from beginning to end; others assume a service of scripture and sermon will be determined locally and therefore provide only a text for the eucharistic action.

## THE ACTION

Recall that in the Pauline formula, "Do this in remembrance of me," the emphasis is on "Do," as a means of *anamnesis.* While a well-wrought text is important, this is but the framework for the central and crucial actions. Although some traditions (particularly Calvinistic and Zwinglian) retain seven actions, in most churches these have been collated into four actions as follows.

1. First the bread and wine are taken by the celebrant, who stands in the stead of the true Host, Jesus Christ. In the past, often the elements were placed on the table (or nearby) before the service began. The first great action was signalled by their uncovering, which was done with great care and dignity, particularly if the table covering was large and required more than one person for its graceful removal.

Increasingly, however, the bread and wine are not on the table when the service begins but are brought from the midst of the congregation by laypersons, who may be designated as "gift bearers." Usually the bread and wine are carried in procession in conjunction with the money offering, the latter being put aside at some convenient place while the eucharistic elements are placed upon the table. The bread is uncovered and the plates readied for the meal. The wine, brought in a pitcher or flagon, is then poured into the eucharistic cup, or chalice.[5] An "offertory prayer" may accompany this action, asking God to take the ordinary things we have brought and by the goodness of divine grace return them to us as more than we have brought, that we may be strengthened by our awareness of Christ's presence and work in our midst. The action itself should be visible and significant without being overblown.[6]

2. The second central action should be precisely what the name "Great Thanksgiving" implies—the greatest prayer of gratitude the church can ever offer, for it expresses above all else our thanksgiving for the redemption of the world in Jesus Christ. Thus the person who gives thanks should embody the centrality of the text, both by being fully visible to the whole congregation and by conveying the dignity and authority that an act so important implies. Unlike the medieval priest and generations of his descendants (including many Protestant clergy) who prayed with their backs to the people, the celebrant should face the congregation across table. The celebrant is there in the stead of Christ the Host; no earthly host would ever entertain at a dinner table while facing toward a wall and away from the guests. The celebrant's voice should be strong, communicating the joy and confidence appropriate to God's people, in whose stead the celebrant also stands at the table.

Let this double representative function of the celebrant at the table be clearly noted, for it has important implications for both the celebrant's inner self-understanding and outward liturgical style. By doing what Jesus did, visibly the celebrant represents to the people Christ, the true Host. By praying in the name of the congregation, the celebrant represents the people to God. Thereby representing both Christ and the congregation, the celebrant in a subtle but very incarnational way reminds all worshipers of the union that exists between Christ and the church.

Some older traditions dictated that the celebrant kneel throughout the Great Prayer, but that posture betokens penitence or abject humility, not gratitude or exultation. Now the celebrant is instructed by most rites to stand through the Great Prayer. It is appropriate to use the ancient posture of prayer common to the Jews and thus to the early church. Technically called the *orans,* or "prayer" position, this stance is alluded to in 1 Timothy 2:8 ("pray, lifting up holy hands"). The arms are not lifted straight upward, but rather are extended away from the body in a kind of embracing gesture, with the hands at shoulder height and shoulder-width apart.[7]

The Great Prayer strikes some worshipers as odd because, unlike most prayer, it includes narration as well as praise and petition. But in the Hebrew tradition of prayer, God is thanked and praised when we retell the story of divine activity. We bless God even in narrative sacred history. The psalms make this amply manifest. In Psalm 148, for example, verses 1-4 are direct praise of God, but verse 5 moves from praise to narration, which characterizes verse 6 also. Direct praise is resumed in verse 7, and narration occurs again in verse 14 before a concluding burst of praise. In this Jewish tradition of blessing God, it is quite natural, therefore, that in the midst of thanksgiving we tell the story of Jesus at table with the disciples. We do not stop praying when we shift to the narrative: "On the same night in which he was betrayed and arrested. . . . " If we think otherwise, we do not know sufficiently well our Hebraic roots.

Nor is it even odd from a Hebraic perspective to engage in certain acts in the midst of this praise-through-narration. Thus at the beginning of the institution narrative, the celebrant may lift the bread and say: "Jesus took bread, gave thanks to you, broke the bread, and gave it to the disciples, saying, 'Take, eat; this is my body which is given for you.' " At this point the bread is replaced on the table unbroken; then the cup is lifted as the narrative continues, "So also after supper Jesus took the cup," and so on.[8]

At the *Epiklesis* the celebrant appropriately gestures toward or touches the loaf and cup while asking that the Spirit make this bread to be for us the body of Christ, and this wine to be for us the blood of Christ. If the prayer goes on to ask the Spirit to come upon the congregation, the celebrant may at that point make an embracing gesture toward all assembled. Then the *orans* posture may be resumed until the close of the prayer.

This use of gesture itself implies a differing stance among the worshipers than often has been the case, for it is assumed that the congregation will notice these gestures; the worshipers are neither to have their heads buried in a liturgy book, nor are they to close their eyes for prayer. The ability to pray with head up and eyes open may at first make people uneasy, or even guilty. It may be necessary to give them explicit permission to do what they may have been very carefully taught not to do. For by those who have neither visual nor hearing loss, the eucharistic prayer is to be both clearly seen and heard. The *anamnesis* is in the doing, to which all should given attention.

Any congregation able to stand through the hymns may also be expected to stand throughout the eucharistic prayer, or at least until the *Sanctus* and *Benedictus qui venit* have been sung or said. With both presider and people assuming the same posture, there is an increased sense of the oneness of the eucharistic community; further, standing more readily connotes joy and thanksgiving than does either sitting or kneeling.

3. After the Great Prayer (and Lord's Prayer, which usually follows) the bread is broken in the third action, known technically as "the fraction." Usually the loaf is broken once, though in small congregations it may be subdivided to provide pieces for each communicant. (In larger congregations, the bread is subdivided at the time of reception.) The broken loaf and the filled chalice are visibly presented before the congregation, and most rites specify one or more appropriate statements to be made at that time.

For example, Paul's words in 1 Corinthians 10:16-17 can be adapted as follows. The celebrant displays the unbroken loaf before the people, saying, "We who are many are one body; for we all partake of the one bread." Then the presider breaks the loaf and says, "When we break the bread, is it not a sharing in the body of Christ?" The bread is then placed on the table and the chalice lifted before the congregation with the words, "The cup of blessing that we bless, is it not a sharing in the blood of Christ?" A brief word of invitation may then be given to the people, such as, "Come; receive with joy these gifts from God." Instructions concerning the manner of reception and the church's policy on intercommunion are better stated at some point in the service prior to the Great Thanksgiving, as they can be unduly intrusive between the fraction and the distribution.

4. Immediately follows the fourth great action: the distribution and reception of the bread and wine. Here practices differ widely. Baptists, Presbyterians, and Disciples, for example, receive in the pew, usually with the bread and the cups being distributed as independent actions by authorized laity. In some places worshipers retain the bread (and later the cup) in the hand until all have been served; then all eat or drink simultaneously as a symbol of eucharistic unity. But others object that such action, being lockstep, conveys artificial or legalistic rather than organic unity; thus they direct each person to eat or drink when served, following the prevalent etiquette at a banquet or large dinner party. The posture of sitting most clearly relates to formal meals in our culture, but the earlier practice of having the worshipers go from their pews to sit at long tables is preferable, though now out of fashion.[9]

Most Episcopalians, Lutherans, and Methodists come forward to a communion rail and are given the elements while kneeling, but in each of these denominations some congregations have followed the practice of post-Vatican II Catholics of receiving while standing. In some places the kneeling rails have been eliminated; in other instances worshipers have the option of kneeling at the rail for personal prayer after having received while standing.

Standing, far from simply being a convenience for those who have difficulty kneeling, is an ancient and venerable practice retained in Eastern Orthodoxy as an affirmation of Christian hope. At the table we meet our risen Lord and believe we shall share by grace in the resurrection; standing connotes the act of being raised from the dead in ways kneeling and sitting do not.

Kneeling was introduced as a form of reception in the West, largely an analogy to respect due a person of great dignity. It was reasoned, for example, that since one knelt when entering the throne room of an earthly monarch, surely one ought even more to kneel out of respect for the Lord of all creation. Kneeling also came to be associated with abject humble penitence in the presence of God, the Judge.

Standing now is preferable to kneeling because both earlier associations have negative implications. The Eucharist is not a penitential rite but an act of thanksgiving. In democracies people rightly object to kneeling before any official of the state. While God is hardly to be brought down to the level of a president or premier, kneeling nevertheless is for us an unaccustomed act and almost automatically brings to mind penitence rather than regard for someone of great dignity. (It may also deter from reception a sizeable number of people, who find it physically difficult to kneel.) On the other hand, it is an accepted practice in most democracies that when a head of state enters the room, all present rise as a sign of respect (though not obeisance), as also in a courtroom all rise at the entrance of the judge.

Except where all eat and drink simultaneously, the order of reception is also a current issue. Historically, the celebrant received communion before the congregation. Behind this were hierarchical principles, evident in medieval paintings that showed lay communicants receiving the Eucharist from a bishop, who received it from the pope, who received it from the hand of God reaching down from heaven! At another point on the theological spectrum, among Protestants the practice was defended on the principle that "you can't give to someone else what you have not first received yourself." Sometimes this was compounded by a specific view of the sacrament as being a means of cleansing from sin; hence the ones who administered the Eucharist needed to be cleansed before beginning the distribution to the congregation.

Today all of these justifications are fraught with problems. But of greater importance is the need to see the Eucharist as a meal; in our society no one hosting a dinner party serves himself or herself before serving the guests. Thus the celebrant, who represents Christ the Host, most appropriately eats and drinks after the congregation, as do servers who assist the presider.

However the sacrament is administered, it should be planned in such a way that it can be carried out with dispatch, yet not haste, and with efficiency, but not regimentation. Both chaotic traffic patterns that leave people confused and embarrassed and ushers or servers who act like abrupt officers of the law can disrupt a reverent reception of the bread and wine. True hospitality should pervade the time of eating and drinking, as it would at any well-hosted meal. For all who receive, the hospitality of the Eucharist in our churches is intended to connote that endlessly vast and ever-welcoming hospitality of heaven, in which those from east and west and north and south are beckoned and greeted warmly by none other than God.

## THE ELEMENTS

In choosing the kind of material things to be eaten and drunk, care should be taken to represent God's good creation with realism and dignity. What is offered to the guests should not have the appearance of being phoney or trivial.

This suggests first the use of a type of bread one might indeed share around a table at home. The plastic-looking wafers so popular in the past convey a kind of unreality to the Eucharist; the wheat wafers introduced in recent years are more breadlike in texture and taste, but still do not connote the sense of sharing that is communicated by a common loaf—or even a series of loaves, such as rounds of pita bread (also known as pocket bread or Sahara bread). Preferable is a whole loaf, perhaps baked at home by a parishioner who also acts as the gift bearer in the first of the fourfold actions. The bread can be light or dark, but it should not be specialized or exotic. The use of cranberry bread or onion-garlic bread also introduces a discordant note to the meal.

The act of breaking the bread should be as natural as the loaf itself. Those who fear a hard-crusted bread will be difficult to break gracefully sometimes slice the loaf 90 percent through as a precaution and then only appear to break the loaf at the fraction.

But pretend-breaking is no better than pretend-bread. If this kind of difficulty is anticipated, the crust around the middle of the loaf may be slightly perforated with an ordinary table fork before the service; the bread will then break readily and naturally. Certainly communicants should not be offered tiny bread cubes, neatly diced from a machine-sliced loaf. This vitiates any breaking action at the table, and the resulting pieces resemble croutons more than regular bread. The bread of Christ's feast should convey, not deny, the deep realities both of the good creation into which we are born by nature and the new creation into which we are incorporated by grace.

Just as a common loaf proclaims our sharing from the one Bread of Life, so also a common cup proclaims our sharing in the True Vine. It is unlikely that congregations accustomed to individual glasses will readily change to a common chalice. Many of the reasons for the intransigence are more emotional than rational. Drinking from a common cup may indeed risk the danger of transmitting certain diseases, but many more are transmitted hand-to-hand than mouth-to-mouth, yet few congregations become urgent about the need to stop shaking hands with the pastor after the service. And despite all current hysteria, HIV is transmitted neither by drinking nor by touching. Still, people are people, which means their irrationalities have to be taken seriously. Forcing a common cup on a congregation that does not want it is less likely to result in an increased sense of commonality than in a decreased participation in the sacrament.

Should a common loaf and common cup be used ceremonially at the table even if the congregation refuses to share from either one during the distribution? On the one hand there are two dangers to such use. First, if no one at all eats and drinks from the common loaf and cup, yet one more level of unreality is introduced into the service. Second, if only the celebrant and perhaps the servers partake from the common elements while everyone else uses wafers and individual cups, an implied hierarchicalism rears its head. On the other side, however, is the importance of visual impression, which we have all too long ignored in liturgy. A whole loaf broken and a cup symbolically extended can in part counteract the individualistic connotations of individual wafers and glasses. On balance, such a symbolic use of the common loaf and cup is probably worth the risk.

A thornier issue has to do with the contents of the cup. Certain denominations, by virtue of a historic belief in total abstinence from alcohol, prohibit the use of wine. In almost any congregation of other denominations there are recovering alcoholics who fear that even the smallest amount of wine will jeopardize their sobriety. Yet Jesus did not use grape juice, which could not be produced before the process of pasteurization was perfected. Not only do many feel wine should be used in imitation of Jesus, but also some denominations adhere to strict rules that only fermented grape wine be used. Since it is not always satisfactory to suggest that those who do not drink wine should receive only the bread during communion, in those denominations without rules allowing fermented wine only, the alternative of having both regular wine and dealcoholized wine or grape juice can be considered. It is at best an awkward expedient, however.

A different, though related, matter has to do with making substitutions for bread or wine due to lack of availability or familiarity. In some areas of the world, wheat, if not totally unavailable, is far less used as a daily food than rice or some other cereal. Is it then legitimate to use rice cakes rather than wheat bread? Similarly, is it allowable to use rice wine where grapes are unknown? Usually such exceptions have been permitted, for not to grant them would impose hardship on churches in such places. Even worse, perhaps, it would introduce great unreality. Better to employ something Jesus did not actually use than to ask people at the Lord's Table to eat or drink something so odd or exotic to them that it cannot be connected with usual meal practices.[10]

So far so good, until these exceptions raise another issue: Why cannot a youth group have a cola and pizza Eucharist at a summer church camp? After all, it is often argued, these are the familiar foods of the youth culture, much more "natural" to them than the usual eucharistic elements. But the usual elements are neither unavailable nor unknown, and the proposed substitutions are very apt to trivialize the sacrament. Novelty, which seems to be the primary motivation to the proposal, does not override the use of the things that more readily connect us with both the practice of Jesus and the tradition of the centuries.

Less well known than the fact that some communicants do not wish to receive fermented wine is the fact that due to allergic reactions some persons cannot tolerate even small quantities of wheat. In such instances suitable substitutes can be made. Where this need is known to exist, a small rice cake can be provided for the person who cannot eat wheat.

In summary, in the choice of eucharistic elements it is necessary to maintain a sensible tension between (a) remaining as close as possible to Jesus' practice without falling into sentimentality, in order that we may remember by doing what he did; and (b) using elements that are neither hurtful nor strange or contrived so that they upset the worshiper or trivialize the eucharistic meal.

Finally, what do we do with the bread and wine that remain after the communion of the congregation? In the Roman Catholic tradition and among some Anglicans, the priest consumes the contents of the chalice; any uneaten bread becomes a part of the reserved sacrament for later consumption and for interim devotions before the Blessed Sacrament by the faithful. Among those at the opposite end of the spectrum, some Protestants routinely dispose of unconsumed elements in a trash can or drain. Each of the groups looks askance at the practices of the other. The Protestants here described consider Catholics to be superstitious if not idolatrous; the Protestants in turn may be regarded as irreverent if not blasphemous by the Catholics.

Between these extremes are many varieties of practices. Some suggest that the excess wine be poured into the earth and the bread be left on the ground for birds to eat. Some church sacristies have a drain that goes directly into the ground, not into a sewer or septic system. Into this drain eucharistic wine and baptismal water are poured. In some congregations, after the service is concluded members of the congregation are invited to return to the table area to finish the elements; in other churches, it is the duty of the communion stewards (who prepare the elements before the service) to gather in the sacristy after the service and themselves consume the remaining elements.

All of this points to two realities. (1) Except among those who simply throw the bread and wine away, there is a sense that whether or not the bread and wine undergo any change, the sacred meaning they proclaim dictates that they be disposed of respectfully. A conviction seems to be emerging that the gifts of creation used by God as a means of divine communication to us should not be disposed of as refuse. (2) However, no agreement has been achieved as to what form a respectful use of the elements shall take, just as there is no agreement as to exactly how the bread and wine function with respect to the Presence of Christ in the feast. Again, however, a consensus is developing that the Presence of Christ is to be seen primarily in the community's action of taking, giving thanks, breaking, and distributing. For these actions the elements are essential, but the actions are themselves the crucial components of *anamnesis* in any celebration of the feast.

## THE FURNISHINGS

The principal furnishing for the Eucharist should above all else be immediately recognizable as a table. It is not intended to represent the kind of altar of animal sacrifice described in Leviticus. (Nor is it a good idea to refer to the table as "the altar," if the Eucharist is to be seen primarily as the church's feast with Christ rather than as a cultic offering up of Christ.) And while in the Middle Ages the eucharistic table came to resemble a sarcophagus, the contemporary counterpart is not intended to represent a tomb—not even an empty one. (In some places the bodies of martyrs were in fact buried within the eucharistic furnishing, so that it indeed was a tomb.)

The design of the eucharistic table should be considered carefully. The table should be dignified and visually significant within the space where it is situated. Since it can be no more than a certain height in order to function well, and since length should be proportionate to height, the table cannot be enlarged at will to be consonant with the room within which it sits. In a very large space, therefore, architectural elements will need to conspire creatively to give the table the visual centrality it merits.

Maximum height is about forty-three inches, but some eucharistic tables are incorrectly made twenty-nine inches high—the same as a dining room table. The difficulty is that no one actually sits at the eucharistic table, and for most celebrants this height is awkward. The kitchen counter, not the table, is the appropriate model for eucharistic table height.

The top (or *mensa*) of many recently constructed eucharistic tables is supported by four legs. This open design visually communicates the clear message: This is a table. Unfortunately it is not without drawbacks. Many people, when in the public eye, unconsciously work out their inevitable anxiety by lower body motion, particularly through their feet. In part that is why the closed pulpit was invented, to say nothing of the closed console behind which television newscasters and talk show hosts sit when on camera! We will make little progress in getting worshipers to look up to view the eucharistic actions if they are distracted by the tight little dance the celebrant is unconsciously doing underneath the table. Therefore, a better design is that of a mensa supported by a central pedestal. Thus the support conceals what is best hidden; yet the furnishing visually connotes "table," since many traditional dining room tables are indeed of the pedestal type.

To enhance its visual message (This is a table), great restraint should be exercised to ensure that this furnishing not become cluttered with extraneous objects. Offering basins and vases should be provided with separate stands or shelves. An open Bible on the Lord's Table is but a decoration, since in that location it is not used for reading. Baptismal bowls so small they can stand on the table should be shunned in favor of ample baptisteries. A cross may be hung above or behind the table rather than being placed on it (even on noneucharistic occasions). At most, two candles may rest on the table, though these can also appropriately stand beside it.[11] In short, the Lord's Table is designed for a meal and should always appear to be in readiness for the celebration of the sacrament. When the Eucharist is celebrated a number of things will be placed on the table, but nothing that is usually there should need to be removed.

Always the table should be evident to the congregation, for by derivation from its function it reminds the worshiper of the Presence of Christ within the liturgical assembly even when the Eucharist is not being celebrated. The table should not be removed at a wedding in order to provide more space for the bridal party, and at a funeral the coffin should be positioned in a way that will not hide the furnishing that witnesses to the living Lord, present in the valley of the shadow and ready always to prepare a table before us in the presence of our great enemy, death. Certainly the table should never serve as a stand for, or be visually overwhelmed by, banks of Christmas poinsettias or lilies at Easter. Everything should enhance the table, and nothing ought to obscure it. Unfortunately, many worship spaces now in existence make this ideal impossible to achieve, but these should warn us of the care that needs to be taken in building design and renovation, lest the mistakes of the past be perpetuated.

Certain coverings characteristically vest the table of the Lord. Chief among these is "the fair linen" that covers the table's top completely. In many traditions its historic design dictates a width the same as that of the mensa and long enough to reach almost to the floor at both ends of the table. Embroidered upon it may be five Greek crosses (four arms of equal length), one at each corner of the mensa and the fifth at the very center of the linen. These are seen to represent the five wounds of the Crucified, and the linen as a whole then symbolically represents the shroud or winding sheet within which the body of the Savior was entombed. But, being risen from the dead, the Lord no longer has need of burial clothes. Indeed, these unneeded symbols of death are transformed into banquet table linens that proclaim the Eucharist to be the Emmaus meal of the risen Christ made known to us in the breaking of the bread.[12]

Cloths are also provided to cover the eucharistic vessels. In the free church tradition, a single large cloth may be placed over the table and all of its vessels both prior to and following the central eucharistic action. In churches that follow more ancient practice, at a minimum a number of linens called "purificators" are used.

These are napkin-like in both design and size, usually with one cross embroidered on each, and especially are used to cover chalices and wipe the lip of the chalice if communicants drink directly from it. A larger, square linen called the corporal may rest on top of the fair linen and directly under the eucharistic vessels. Other linens include the pall (not to be confused with the coffin vestment of the same name), the veil, and the burse; these are used less frequently than formerly, and specific information about them is readily found in eucharistic manuals published by those denominations that consider them standard.

Some tables also use frontals or frontlets—paraments usually in the color of the liturgical season and bearing symbols related to it. Except in the case of the "Laudian" or "Jacobean" frontal, these do not totally cover the table and hence do not conceal its true function. The very ample Laudian style, which falls to the floor on all sides, may appropriately signal the occurrence of the Great Fifty Days of Easter or the Twelve Days of Christmas; but any more extended use of it than this simply obscures the fact that underneath this vesture is a real table, conveying to us the joy and generosity of a real meal.

Contemporary eucharistic vessels themselves should connote dignity and grace without ostentation. Equally inapproriate are poorly designed vessels of recent vintage (made of plastic, aluminum, and even paperboard) and the solid gold, jewel-encrusted extravagances of yesteryear. By contrast, chalices, flagons, and plates (or patens) can be made by skilled artists from silver, pewter, pottery, or glass.

Most problematic in design are the individual containers required by those who wish not to use the common chalice. The familiar little glass cups have given rise to many an irreverent remark about "shot glasses"; still, they are preferable to their flimsy-looking plastic replacements—to say nothing of the paper version that resembles an individual container for coffee cream, complete with double cardboard lids between which rests a tiny piece of something that poses as bread but is not.

An innovation that is more satisfying, but probably not practical except in small congregations, consists of using small pottery cups without handles. When approaching the Lord's

Table, each communicant takes from a convenient stand an empty cup. Into this the server pours a bit of wine from a chalice equipped with a pouring lip. After reception, the cups are placed on another stand as communicants return to their seats.

The vesture of celebrants and servers is too complex a matter to treat here. Three comments must suffice: (1) Vestments by their historic longevity can connect us with the heritage of the church and remind us of generations of Christians before similarly attired, in contrast to the rapidly changing dictates of the world of fashion in street wear. Still, virtually all the vestments we use are modifications and conservations of what once was street wear (or more formal court attire) and are not attempts to replicate the priestly vestments of the Judaic Temple. (2) Particular kinds of clothing are by no means part and parcel of eucharistic celebration, though in some ecclesiastical traditions it may appear otherwise. Vestments may put a psychological stumbling block before those unaccustomed to them, but they can add grace and dignity and—like a pedestal table—conceal distracting mannerisms on the part of the celebrant. (3) Certain vestments are reserved according to status or function—only the clergy wear stoles, for these are badges of ordination; only the celebrant wears a chasuble. But other forms of vesture are unrestricted. Lay servers assisting in the liturgy may wear cassock and surplice or cotta, or a contemporary alb with cincture.

All furnishings should be harmonious with all others and generally consonant with the architectural style of the site. An ill-considered mixture of styles can be jarring or even humorous, even if each component is well designed and pleasing on its own. For Christ's feast with the church, the same aesthetic care should be taken as would be employed in planning the ambience of a fine secular banquet; at the same time, however, aesthetic snobbery and fussiness should be shunned. This presents a challenge that too often goes unnoticed: A simple dignity, unstudied in appearance, is more difficult to achieve than an obvious and intrusive striving after elegance or contrived effect.[13]

## THE PEOPLE

A formula that is commonplace in some circles is mystifying or even infuriating in others—namely, this: "The Eucharist is for the baptized." To some this sounds like a narrow restrictiveness. If the Eucharist proclaims the graciousness of God, and if the presence of the risen Lord in the breaking of the bread is capable of transforming us more and more to bring us into conformity with Christ's new creation, why not open the table to one and all, baptized or not? The answer lies in the positive assertions being made by the statement rather than in what may be perceived as narrow exclusivism.

First, the affirmation that the Eucharist is for the baptized is to take the focus from our action (and worthiness or lack thereof) and to place the focus on God's grace. Baptism is God's gift to us, unworthy though we may be to become a part of a divinely initiated covenant community. The people of the Table are the same people to whom grace has been proclaimed at the Font. If this is not affirmed, an unfortunate sorting out process occurs such that the people at the table are welcome there by virtue of something other than divine goodness.

Usually that something other has been connected to human works and has resulted in agonizing personal decisions about whether to receive the sacrament. The old Anglican formula of invitation to the table was well intended by those who wrote it, but its consequences were often horrific: "Ye that do truly and earnestly repent you of your sins. . . . " But, asked the diligent communicant, "How true and earnest am I? Sure, I want to be a better person. But maybe I am only kidding myself. I so readily fall into doing the very thing I resolve not to do. Perhaps I had better stay away. My repentence is not sufficiently true and earnest." The invitation continued, " . . . and are in love and charity with your neighbors. . . . " And the potential communicant's conscience remonstrated: "I've done my best to make up with Mr. Grouchy down the street, and he still refuses to speak to me. Then there's Mrs. Contentious, who picks a fight at every opportunity. And as to my unreasonable and exploitative employer who berates me daily. . . . So I really am not in love and charity with my neighbors, and I cannot take communion."

In comparison to this, the statement that the Eucharist is for the baptized is a liberating word without being an excuse for license. Baptism indeed makes moral and ethical demands on us, but to these nothing is added as an obligation before communion. God willingly feeds those to whom God gives life; and the Eucharist, far from being a reward to the superpious, is an aid to us as we work out the implications of our baptismal covenant responsibility.

Second, and closely related, while concrete and objective categories can be confining, abstract and subjective ones frequently are more so. Often those who prefer not to address "the baptized" instead invite "all those who love and serve the Lord." The formulation is different from that of the old Anglican invitation, but it is no less troublesome. Confronted with such an "invitation," I must ask, "But do I really love the Lord? I try to. I want to. But do I actually succeed? On what basis do I decide the answer? As to service, there are so many other things I also must serve, and so often even my best efforts are self-serving. Is my dedication to God truly service? How can I tell?" Thus the invitation that is intended to be inclusive is rather instead a bother to the sensitive conscience. I can know for certain that I have been baptized. As to whether I truly love and serve the Lord, God alone knows. Hence I must be much more troubled and tentative about approaching the table—unless I am content to be merely superficial.

Third, to say that our baptism is our admission to the Table is to say that a more restrictive denominationalism is not the crucial factor. There are complexities to this matter as they relate to inter-communion; these will be dealt with in the next chapter, and some of these seem to deny what the formula asserts. But at its root, to assert that those who are baptized are welcomed at the eucharistic table is to place emphasis on the unity of Christ's people, given to us by none other than God. The oneness of our common initiation by grace, not any lesser compatibility based on denominational association, binds us at the deepest possible level. We eat together at the Lord's Table not because we are devout Lutherans or diligent Anglicans or conscientious

Presbyterians but because we are God's people, so identified by the water of the font.

Then the question arises: Is the Eucharist for all who have been thus baptized, or only for those who have also been confirmed or made some parallel act of commitment at a later age? The Orthodox have always granted communion to infants and children, but until recently both Roman Catholics and most Protestants have barred from communion baptized persons for a number of years beyond infancy. The barriers are now being reconsidered—particularly where they were erected out of the conviction that the Eucharist must be rationally understood before it can be rightly received. But denominational policies vary greatly, and within some denominations more than one practice is sanctioned. At best we can raise here these crucial questions: Do we indeed believe that the Eucharist is a means that facilitates the growth of faith rather than a reward for faith achieved? Do we indeed believe that persons of all ages can know (even if in different ways and to various degrees) the presence of the risen Christ? Do we also believe that the Eucharist is more to be experienced than explained? And how do the barriers we have placed around the table concerning the age of communicants stand up against our answers to these questions?[14]

Finally, the assertion that the Eucharist is for the baptized is a statement about the sacrament itself as well as about the people who receive it. The Eucharist is more than the Sunday morning coffee hour. Baptism proclaims who we really are as the covenanted people of God, set apart for service; in ways that coffee and pastry are unable to do, the Eucharist strengthens and motivates us to be who we are.

The celebration of the Eucharist, then, is a means of nourishing and thus equipping for ministry the covenanted (baptized) people of God, lay and clergy together. Any vital celebration of the sacrament must take seriously this ecclesiological dimension and its implications for evangelical life and service. The breadth of this dimension will occupy our attention in the final chapter.

CHAPTER SEVEN

# "THAT MY HOUSE MAY BE FILLED"

In Jesus' story of the great dinner, the householder sends a servant with the instruction, "Go out at once into the streets and lanes of the town and bring in the poor, the crippled, the blind, and the lame." But when this is accomplished there is still room; so the householder further commands: "Go out into the roads and the lanes, and compel people to come in, so that my house may be filled" (Luke 14:15-24). The heavenly banquet hall is vast, and God desires urgently that it be filled, for our Maker has an expansive nature, and the sharing of good things is at the center of divine creative love.

Too often the church has engaged in emptying out the house, or at least being content with the current guest list, contrary to the whole meaning of the Eucharist. What does it imply for the church if indeed we are charged with ensuring that God's house be filled for the feast? We shall look at the implications under three headings: congregational, ecumenical, and evangelical.

## FILLING GOD'S HOUSE CONGREGATIONALLY

We take it for granted that the Eucharist at a minimum is open to all within the congregation who wish to receive. In fact, often it is open only to those who are able to attend—which is not the same as those who want to attend. Many willingly absent themselves for a variety of reasons—good or not—but others are unwillingly absent due to various limitations. Those in the first group need a different understanding of the sacrament, particularly if they stay away because they feel unworthy, but those in the latter group suffer a kind of unintended excommunication that cries out for correction.

The range of difficulties that prevents attendance may be great, from regular employment at the stated times of worship to an inability to reach the place of worship due to physical limitations. Part of the problem in the latter category may be remedied by making the worship space accessible by wheelchair. But other persons may be confined to their homes, while being otherwise alert with normal attention spans. Others may be critically ill, confined to an intensive care unit with strictly regulated visitation times of short duration. Still others, whether at home or in medical facilities, may suffer chronic mental impairment or senility. A multitude of other possibilities makes evident how diverse is the spectrum of those who cannot attend the congregational service. All cannot be ministered to alike. But no one loses membership in a Christian congregation by virtue of physical or mental difficulty; and to the extent possible, all should be included in the congregation's eucharistic fellowship.

In most parishes, those who are regularly absent due to work schedules or other inhibiting difficulties (such as continuous care for family members who are ill) are simply left to their own devices out of lack of awareness and imagination, rather than out of malice. Communion of the sick and shut-in, on the other hand, usually is attended to, but is delegated to the pastor; thus it is often done on a schedule unrelated to the congregation's Eucharist—that is, at the mutual convenience of clergy and communicants. Certainly systematic pastoral calling on such persons is expected, and these visits may include the Lord's Supper on occasion. But without alternative practices, undesirable consequences can occur. The notion that the Eucharist is primarily an individualistic act of piety is reinforced, a more general sense of congregational unity is eroded, and the ministry of the laity one to another is greatly obscured.

Consider an alternative: As an extension of the congregation's Eucharist, lay members take from the Lord's Table portions of bread and wine to be shared that same day with absent members who would attend except for the kinds of difficulties noted above. The names of those to be thus included in the communion may be announced in the congregation's liturgy, with prayers said specifically for them. The kind of service of distribution used in each instance can vary according to the circumstances but will emphasize the unity and common responsibility of all within the congregation. Those who carry the elements to the absent will be well-trained in their ministry.

If the whole concept seems odd, probably it is due to our overly clerical conception of the church. Only the clergy, we suppose, have the "right" to administer the Eucharist. Certainly there are good reasons for restricting the function of presiding at the table to persons duly authorized by their churches, usually through ordination, but presiding should be distinguished from distributing, as it already is in many churches during the Sunday morning celebration. In traditions as diverse as Roman Catholic and Baptist, the priest or pastor presides at the table, but authorized laity may distribute the elements throughout the church building. The proposal for lay administration outside of the church building is but an extension of this principle of lay eucharistic ministry.

Furthermore, the practice of extending the Eucharist to the unwillingly absent is of ancient and venerable origin. Already in the second century, Justin Martyr reported that after the congregation has received the bread and wine "they are sent to the absent by the deacons."[1] Much further beyond that, however, lies the Hebraic conception of the unity of the covenant people in eating and drinking. In Nehemiah 8, the people hear read to them a newly recovered scroll of scripture and listen also to its interpretation by their leaders. Then they are exhorted to feast, to "eat the fat and drink sweet wine," but it is further stipulated that they are to "send portions of them to those for whom nothing is prepared" (8:10). Certain traditional Passover legislation also made provision for the inclusion of all the faithful. While these Hebraic precedents should not be seen as antecedents of the later Christian distribution of the Eucharist to the absent, neither can their spirit of communal sharing within the covenant household be regarded as irrelevant.

Consider what happens when sharing with the unwillingly

absent does not occur. Those recently prevented from attending corporate worship will be remembered in prayer by the congregation for a time, and the ill likely will have their names posted on a bulletin board or listed in a parish publication. But for those unable to attend over a period of months or years, congregational awareness is apt to decrease, particularly in a parish with a transient membership. Ultimately the roll of the unwillingly absent becomes the roll of the unknown—unknown even to many active members. This roll then may be ignored—or worse, no longer made available. Thereafter, only longtime friends, family members, and the clergy maintain contact with the unwillingly absent.

Can worshipers assembled on Sunday have a true sense of Christian community when, in fact, members of that community are thus hidden from the corporate consciousness? To turn the coin over, how do those who cannot attend maintain any real sense of being a living part of a community of faith when their contact with the members of the congregation is so restricted? Often at the death of someone who was active and vibrant for half a century and then incapacitated for a decade, the funeral is attended only by the family and close friends because no one in the congregation any longer remembers the deceased. This is a sore judgment upon the church as a household of communion with Christ and of concern for one another.

In Appendix 1, pages 155-59, is a proposed rite with general instructions and particular acts done within the congregational service and at the places of distribution. You may wish to refer to this rite now and throughout the remainder of this section of the chapter.

What is proposed here is not an easy way out for the clergy, even though pastors thereby may have fewer communion calls to make. Instead this proposal implies careful preparation, training, and constant monitoring. Before a plan for the proposed program can be devised and implemented, it is necessary to emphasize three assumptions:

1. The Eucharist is at heart a congregational act, not an act of individual piety done in isolation from the community of faith.

2. Insofar as possible, the communicants should include all who wish to receive.
3. Ministering to the unwillingly absent is part of the ministry of the laity, not something reserved to the clergy.

The second assumption is more likely to be granted immediately than the first and third; even so, this may not imply that any connection is seen between the timing of the Sunday Eucharist and the communion of those who cannot attend that service. For so long have the two events been separated that any attempt to unite them may at first seem odd, or at least unnecessary. The first and third assumptions may engender a stimulating and healthy controversy about the nature of the sacrament and the role of the ordained within the church.

Discussion and formulation of local policies about distribution after the parish Eucharist should be as broadly based as possible—beginning, most likely, in small committees charged with planning worship and ministering to those who cannot attend services, and moving on through usual channels to the chief policy group of the congregation. Once a policy is established, it should be disseminated by various modes of teaching: study groups, sermons, and discussions in publications. As in all such cases of education, a variety of approaches and techniques well-spaced over a long period will avail more than the "one-time blitz" approach, upon which the contemporary church tends to rely all too heavily.

Care needs to be taken as to how lay servers of the bread and wine are to be selected and assigned. What is not needed is a coterie of servers who become elitist and monopolistic. Probably, therefore, a rotation system is advisable, such that servers function for a maximum term, perhaps in "classes" to achieve continuity. For example, suppose it is determined that a church needs nine teams of two each to serve its needs, and that each person should act in this capacity for a maximum of three years. At the end of Year A, six persons would be rotated off, another six at the end of Year B, and the remainder at the close of Year C. Thus there would always be a majority of experienced persons who guide the newly selected. Systematic rotation has three great advantages: (1) It will aid in recruitment, since many potential servers fear accepting the responsibility lest it be theirs "until death us do part," and since they will know they can draw on the experience of their fellow servers. (2) Rotation allows for a graceful exit of those whose service, for one reason or another, has become unsatisfactory. (3) Rotation allows a great number within the congregation the opportunity of service (thereby reducing the danger that a clique mentality will develop) and nurtures a broader fellowship with those absent.

Servers should go out at least two-by-two, with one person of each team being experienced in the program. It is tempting to employ spouses as teams, since this simplifies the logistics of pairing and transportation. But too great a reliance on this pattern creates more problems than it solves. Consider: Is distributing communion a marital function? How are single persons then to feel fully a part of this congregational act (or even of the congregation that thinks in this constricted way)? Further, if two persons not of the same family form a visitation team, this both increases the representative nature of the visit and allows unrelated members of the congregation to become more fully acquainted with one another as they minister together.

For the same kind of logistical reasons, it is tempting for family members or close friends of those unable to attend to be selected as their visitation teams. But this does little to enhance congregational interaction or familiarity between newer members and those who are absent over a long period; and it can create an unwarranted equation of biological family to spiritual family. It is also wise to decide as a matter of policy whether the same teams should always visit the same people. There are advantages both to familiarity and to alternation. Perhaps a maximum number of visits by a particular serving team to the same person should be set.

Just as potential servers need to be identified, so also do potential communicants. How often shall they be visited—each time there is a parish Eucharist? The answer may vary from person to person, based on their own past frequency of reception or the circumstances of their confinement. Particularly if eucharistic frequency in the Sunday service has increased significantly since the person became unable to attend, the current schedule and previous personal patterns of reception may be out of phase. But make no snap judgments on this matter based on age! Too often one hears statements such as, "Well, our elderly members will not readily adapt to a schedule of more frequent communion than they grew up knowing." In truth, it is not usually the elderly who are the most resistant to change, but the middle-aged (which I can confidently assert, being among that number myself).

Recently I overheard a three-generation family discussing the adoption of a weekly Eucharist in their Lutheran congregation. The middle generation, aged early fifties, complained about this "innovation" and questioned its value. Their children, young adults, were much more positive. Then came the comments of the grandmother, aged eighty-five: "Well, I think it's just grand. Sure we didn't do it that way years ago. So what?" Her husband nodded enthusiastic agreement. How representative of life freed from stereotypes! Granted, some elderly persons become increasingly inflexible, but most, having lived long enough to see all kinds of change, and having grown increasingly secure with maturity, become more supple in their senior years than they were in the decades immediately preceding. The church does well not to underestimate the positive transforming effect age can have upon us.

Just as assumptions should not be made about the elderly, so also certain things should not be taken for granted about those without full mental capacity. Our pervasive rationalistic tendencies cause us readily to excommunicate persons on the basis of mental incompetence. If they cannot "understand" the sacrament, they should not have it! But surely our survey of the intellectual history of the sacrament demonstrates that often those who can explain it best actually understand it least. More important, it is possible that God has given us the sacraments as one means of communicating with us through taste, sight, sound, smell, and touch when the more rational faculties fail us—whether through permanent mental incapacity or through those temporary psychological traumas in life that afflict us all from time to time.

Surely it is by now apparent that operating such a program of eucharistic visitation will require a great deal of coordination and record keeping. It will necessitate contacting servers to determine their availability for specific dates as well as calling potential communicants to arrange times for visits. Do not overlook the possibility that such details may be done not by overworked parish staff members or already overextended laity but by one or more of the persons to be visited by the serving teams. Some who are housebound are quite able and eager to do tasks such as telephoning and record-keeping; but they are rarely asked, since their inability to attend puts them on the margins where we fail to notice them, let alone see their potential as volunteer workers. Here is an opportunity that enables them to contribute to the program as well as to receive its benefits.

Extending the Eucharist to all who wish to receive in the way suggested here has the potential both to fill God's banquet table more adequately and to enhance the appreciation of the Supper by all who partake of it. Certainly the unintentionally excommunicated will benefit greatly from being included. But likely those who distribute the bread and wine will themselves come to an even greater appreciation of the sacrament as they serve it to others. Not least, the whole congregation should thereby be enabled to see itself more readily as a cohesive body rather than simply a conglomeration of those individuals who happen to show up on a given Sunday.

## FILLING GOD'S HOUSE ECUMENICALLY

Of equal concern but greater complexity is the need for all Christians to be able to gather around a single board on earth, as surely they expect to do in heaven. Currently divisions of all kinds exist. Among some groups, the Supper is seen so strictly as the ratification of a congregational covenant of faith that even visiting members of other congregations of the same denomination are not welcome to receive communion. In many other instances, reception of the bread and wine is limited to members in good standing of the same denomination and, perhaps, certain other denominations with which that denomination has formal accords on inter-communion. In some cases such exclusion is based on a desire for doctrinal agreement or moral rectitude; in other instances, it has to do with traditions about ordination and the "invalidity" of the sacrament unless the celebrant's ordination is fully recognized. Of late, some groups that have accepted the ordination of other groups have backed away from such acceptance if the ordained person is female, or even if the other denomination simply recognizes the ordination of women.[2]

But even those of us who boast an open communion table practice subtle kinds of excommunication in fact, even if unwittingly and unwillingly. Because many congregations closely reflect local housing patterns, diversity in racial and cultural composition often is distressingly restricted to a narrow band of socioeconomic levels. What is to be done by Christians of good will who wish to see it otherwise?

First, we must learn to acknowledge an uncomfortable tension. If we take seriously our common baptism (as do most of the groups that nevertheless exclude other baptized Christians), we can readily pontificate: "We are one through baptism; so there is no reason why we can't all gather at the same table. Let's just do it, that's all." If the complexities of exclusion are explored no more fully than that, the exclusion appears to be simply a matter of incivility—the ecclesiastical version of bad manners.

On the other hand, if the reality of human sin and the intransigence of institutions to change is taken too fatalistically, all hope of reform may simply be surrendered. "It is all so complicated and of such long standing; there is nothing we can do. They [meaning church officials in Rome or Louisville or Canterbury or Nairobi or Rio] decide on these things; and they will never change." Between optimistic oversimplicity and pessimistic acquiescence, Christians—clergy and laity—must seek a middle way or ways.

At the level of church legislation forbidding inter-communion there are two ways, either of which can be defended and practiced with integrity. One is what can be called "the agony of exclusion" theory. In this view members of denominations that exclude each other should obey the rule books but at the same time should frequently attend services in which they cannot fully take part. The pain of seeing in the congregation practicing Christians who cannot be invited to share the bread and cup should, according to this view, motivate a drive to demand reforms in the law. The second practice can be called "the legal lag" theory. The operating assumption is that church law lags behind church practice. Therefore, the best tactic is to break the exclusionary laws so often that eventually those laws will be rescinded because the will to enforce them no longer exists.

There may well be other approaches, equally valid. What surely is not valid is an easy acceptance of the status quo of exclusionary church law. If we agree that God has made us one and equal in baptism, and if we believe that God's house should be filled—with those who fill it eating in the same banquet hall, not in private dining rooms—then an insistent drive toward full inter-communion between Christian denominations is mandatory. What appears to be a diminution in recent years of ecumenical intensity is hardly a good sign. Patient but determined movement is essential.

The achievement of eucharistic tables within a single denomination that are thoroughly representative of that denomination's membership is at once easier and more difficult. It is easier in that the exclusion is in fact contrary to church law. Those who are recognized members of a denomination are to be welcomed at the table in any of its congregations (except in those churches that regard the Supper to be strictly closed to all except members of a single communicating congregation). On the other hand, habits of informal discrimination based on racial identity, ethnicity, social status, educational achievement, economic level, and the like are much harder to change than are church laws. There is no ecclesiastical equivalent of forced bussing. Furthermore, some minority groups, fearing absorption into the dominant culture, advocate the maintenance of distinct congregations as a means of preserving a heritage they fear may be destroyed by inclusivism.

In such circumstances, joint eucharistic fellowships will need to be created with deliberation and determination. This may be done by two congregations of differing composition deciding to have a joint Eucharist from time to time; or denominational governing bodies or agencies may sponsor events for several congregations of differing composition. Likely only then will it be possible for similar events to occur between congregations of differing denominations, even if inter-communion among them poses no formal problems of breaking church law. That is, a joint eucharistic celebration by white, black, and Korean Presbyterians and Methodists is unlikely (though not to be discouraged) until similar observances have already been experienced in each denomination separately.

The problem is complicated, of course, by differing communion customs. In terms of familiarity with a particular rite and manner of distribution, for example, there will be less commonality between a white Evangelical Lutheran Church of America (ELCA) congregation and a white United Church of Christ (UCC) congregation than between a white ELCA congregation and a black Episcopal congregation, on the one hand, or a black UCC congregation and a Korean Presbyterian congregation on the other. Lutherans and Episcopalians both are accustomed to kneeling at a rail and drinking from a common chalice, while Presbyterian and UCC congregations are used to being served individual cups in their pews.

Nor should the goal of inter-communion be seen as an attempt to impose one rite or form on everyone. Practices can well continue to vary within the great household of faith—and may even become further diversified. What cannot continue in the name of Christ is isolation and exclusion, whether legal or de facto. One people at one table is essential on the way toward fulfilling the charge that "my house may be filled."

## FILLING GOD'S HOUSE EVANGELICALLY

*Evangel* means "good news." Surely there is no better news than this: God is with us and graciously draws us into the great banquet hall, where all may be sustained. Further, this good news, as it is represented in the eucharistic feast, is intended to reveal to us certain good news about God's intention for our world. The servant of the host in Jesus' story is commanded to bring to the banquet "the poor, the crippled, the blind, the lame"—that is, those usually overlooked or discriminated against. The intention is not that these should have one good evening to remember and then be sent back to life as it was before. This is a parable about the kingdom of God, so that those who were the victims of society are vindicated. For them a new era is instituted, and wholeness is given as a right where inferiority had prevailed as an unquestioned custom.

Luther insisted that at the Eucharist the veil before our eyes, which distorts our grasp of reality, is lifted, so that we see things as they truly are. And this is how they truly are. At the feast in heaven, God shares generously and openly with all who attend. Furthermore, the church is instructed by Jesus to pray continually "your will be done on earth as it is in heaven." Therefore the church is called both to announce and to enact how things are with God. The discomfort this mission brings explains in part why we have been far too willing to see the Eucharist as a repetition of events in the upper room on the night of Jesus' betrayal and arrest, and far too unwilling to see the Eucharist as the announcement and anticipation in the church of the Great Supper in heaven. To declare in word and deed how things really are from God's perspective is the church's basic evangelical task, no matter how uncomfortable that assignment may make us.

Christians are thus commissioned to challenge unjust and destructive systems taken for granted in the way the world is usually viewed. This we may look at on three levels.

1. As already indicated, the guest list at the heavenly banquet has vast implications for the treatment of persons on earth—particularly for those persons in society most readily overlooked, abused, or exploited. But in our discussion of creation in chapter 1, we noted how readily a view that is too human-centered ignores God's regard for the rest of creation.

2. Therefore, in addition to the guest list, it is necessary that we

take seriously the meal itself. Bread and wine come from the things of earth: wheat and grapes. These in turn depend on a healthy planet, and one not devastated. Suppose that, in a well-meaning attempt to provide justly for the physical welfare of all the people now on earth, we ruin the earth itself; then we have suffered from a short-sighted anthropocentrism of catastrophic proportions both for humanity and for all else on the planet. Is there any way to prevent this?

3. From a Christian perspective, our best chance for avoiding such disaster is to take seriously not only the guest list and the meal itself, but also the very name given to the event: the Eucharist. Only through a profound thanksgiving to God in all things are we apt to find both a proper view of life and a sufficiently strong motivation to act practically and readily. Such gratitude is not easily found, as Jesus reminded us in the story of the ten whom he healed; only one in ten returned to give thanks, and that was a Samaritan—someone generally assumed to be too spiritually obtuse to get things right (Luke 17:11-19). In profound and continual thanksgiving, the evangelical note is sounded most clearly. In the midst of a spiritually forgetful society, the Eucharist is an enacted reminder of the Pauline injunction to "rejoice always, pray without ceasing, give thanks in all circumstances; for this is the will of God in Christ Jesus for you" (1 Thess. 5:16-18).

Thanksgiving to God is no panacea—if for no other reason than that we are capable of distorting even that. (Likely the nine who did not return to thank Jesus for their healing would have replied to his criticism of their inaction by saying, "Oh, but we felt thankful inwardly.") Still, is there any cure for greed and an insatiable lust for what we don't have except a grateful recognition of what we do have? Sharing—which above all the Eucharist instructs us in—is impossible so long as we think we do not have enough. Generosity becomes possible only with the thankful awareness—indeed the good news—that God has given us more than enough. Then the door is opened that allows us to recognize the genuine needs of others and to know that God's creation is intended to be a commonwealth in the literal sense.

But will this evangelical word of God's goodness have

universal appeal? Not likely, if Jesus is to be believed. Not only did nine out of ten of those healed by Jesus fail to return in thanksgiving, but also Jesus' story of the great feast has in it an annoying motif we have thus far neglected to mention: the servant was sent out to bring in guests that the house might be filled because those who were first invited refused to come. The final sentence of the parable is distressingly harsh. Says the host, "None of those who were invited will taste my dinner." Why not? Because the evangel demands of us a positive and active response. Commitment is presumed.

Those of whom Jesus said that they would not taste the feast were the ones who would not commit themselves to acceptance of the invitation as a priority. Something else—inspecting the newly purchased real estate, trying out the new oxen, enjoying personal privacy—took first place and prevented commitment. Acceptance of the invitation to the feast implies commitment, responsibility, and accountability. If what is proclaimed in the Eucharist is to be an evangelical word to the world, those who eat and drink together will at a minimum demonstrate an unflagging devotion to God's purpose. Why would anyone outside of the church take us seriously otherwise? In the absence of perfection (which we cannot claim), commitment is crucial.

Assume it is true that precisely because commitment is assumed our evangelical witness will not be universally appealing. Is there any reason then to suspect that our witness will appeal to anyone at all? If we are faithful, surely that witness will effectively address the excluded of society and those who stand with them in the struggle for justice and a right stewardship of creation. To those who believe themselves to be free, God's word of invitation often sounds like bad news; to those who know themselves to be bound, the gospel is a word that brings the promise of authentic freedom.

To the privileged, words like *responsibility* and *commitment to God* can be harsh and intimidating. But to those who have had to obey oppressive forces within society that have kept them down, serving a good and righteous God who desires the welfare of all people will more readily be seen as release and renewal. These may freely and gladly come when given an authentic opportunity to enter into the banquet hall of divine grace, even as did those from the lanes and streets in Jesus' story.

The unending task of the eucharistic community is to announce authentically the opportunity of freedom in Christ for all people, and to ratify that announcement with persuasive action, that God's house may be filled. But once more, stress must be put on the term *eucharistic community*. If commitment is the demand the truly evangelical church must announce, community is the reality the truly evangelical church is challenged to incarnate.

Surely one of the greatest gifts the church has to offer the world is the gift of community. We live in an age increasingly fractured and separated. Our alienation is expedited by modern modes of travel, by frantic schedules imposed upon us in a complex social order, by ideologies that dispose us to regard those who differ from us with suspicion if not outright hostility. The possibilities for destructive conflict in a fragmented world armed with nuclear technology are too gruesome to contemplate deeply enough for us to be grasped by the magnitude of the danger. Yet we can never escape the menacing presence of those possibilities. Space travel has taught us that the earth is but a global village, and daily news reports alarmingly reveal just how chaotic village life can be.

Christians understandably yearn to set things right—and are becoming more and more frustrated by an apparent inability to do just that. It is laudable for the church to seek to transform individual legislators and world leaders into better politicians and diplomats, and equally commendable for the church to bring moral influences to bear on the aggregate powers that be. But increasingly it is dawning upon us that the church is not Congress or Parliament or the General Assembly of the United Nations. The church is congregations gathered around the Table of the Lord. Incompletely understood, that realization can cause us to sink into an abyss of helplessness and hopelessness. The sea is so vast, and our boat is so small! But if we truly understand who we are, suddenly we begin to realize that we have an opportunity to influence the world more profoundly than we have imagined.

The church has the potential to be a model of community for a fractured social order—one of the few models, it seems, and one with congregations literally in millions of places around the world. Thus positioned, the church has the potential to show society what community is and the power to make the world homesick for the community it has too readily surrendered—or has never known. This potential will not be realized so long as the churches are at odds with each other, or so long as each congregation sees itself internally not as a community of service gathered around a table but as a commissary to which hungry individuals come for personal provision and then leave, essentially unaffected by anything except their own perception of faith.

If the contemporary church would give our perplexed society a valuable and enduring gift, let it be the gift of modelling true community. This means first grasping what Christians once firmly held but have allowed to slip away or to become individualistic and even trivial: a clear vision of the Great Feast in heaven.

It is tragically ironic that for many earnest contemporary Christians, heaven is dismissed as something that distracts us from reshaping life on earth. In this view, heaven functions as an escape hatch, a refuge for those who refuse to deal with practical realities. This is a grievously debased understanding of heaven—and one alien to New Testament teaching. For the first Christians, heaven was a hope secured by the promise of the faithful God—a hope to be instituted already on earth of the grace of God at work in the community of the faithful; for this reason the church perpetually prayed, "Your kingdom come, your will be done on earth as it is in heaven." The church still so prays without unceasing—but often uncomprehending of the meaning of the petition. These are no idle words spoken in between the affirmation of the holiness of God's name and the petition for daily bread. They are instead a profound assertion of the coherence of divine righteousness and daily life.

The church that would proclaim true and enduring good news to the world necessarily first grasps the vision of the Great Feast in heaven and prays and labors endlessly for the effecting of feasts of love on earth, radiating from the Table of the Lord. "Labors endlessly" does not imply we shall achieve this by human effort alone. Community is given by God, but it is never given magically nor imposed upon the unwilling. Those who were compelled to come to the feast in Jesus' parable were not the ones who had declined the invitation.

Laboring endlessly means, rather, this: So much in human nature seems to override commonality and to work for splintering that people of faith are called to resist deliberately and aggressively all inclination to isolate persons from persons, classes from classes, races from races, and nations from nations. Apart from conscious and courageous decisions to seek out and to extend community, nothing important or lasting is likely to happen. Just as the gracious God seeks us, luring us to a sumptuous banquet at a common board, so also we are called to embrace divinely given community by answering the invitation in order that God's house may be filled—not merely by us, but by all whom God has made and longs to reunite in a feast perpetual.

# EPILOGUE

With a feast far more grand than Babette could ever have imagined for the little community of believers on the coast of Jutland, the risen Lord comes to the church. Like the men and women of that village, we often fail to recognize who it is that stands in our presence, offering up everything for our benefit. Like Mary Magdalene, we mistake him for the gardener; or like Cleopas and his companion on their way to Emmaus, we comprehend nothing at all, finding only mystification where divine mystery awaits discovery.

Many who come to the table set themselves against it, as did Babette's guests, determined even before they arrive not to enjoy the meal, no matter what. Religion as they see it is very serious business—and often close to being grim. These well-meaning but ill-informed dinner guests require an interpreter—their counterpart of the decorated military officer—who can speak to them with authority and attest to the unique and splendid glory of the feast.

The task of just such interpretation is committed to the preachers and teachers of the church. Unless they stand and speak clearly, old misconceptions will prevail; the sacrament will continue to be viewed as a funeral for poor Jesus rather than the wedding supper of the victorious Lamb. How great an opportunity and responsibility is thus given to those teachers and preachers of Christ's flock. They can facilitate the transformation of a grudging obligation to "Do this" because Jesus commanded it into joyful actions of taking, giving thanks, breaking, and sharing in the presence of the risen One.

And who are these preachers and teachers? They are not only the ordained or the salaried educators. They are not even only those recruited to work as volunteers in the formal educational program of the congregation. These preachers and teachers are any who have themselves discovered new meaning in the sacramental meal, who have found there a fresher and deeper way of looking at the world God has given us, who have sensed there the call to service and justice on behalf of everything the Creator has made. When these share with others the truth they have themselves perceived, then the whole company of the faithful will find refreshment. Long-standing grudges will be forgiven through the table fellowship, new pleasures will be enjoyed in company with one another, and frail old spiritual bodies will dance in the village street. Then the Host of the table will be heard to declare: "Behold, I am making all things new. The old has passed away. The new is already in your midst."

Amen. Come, Lord Jesus!

# APPENDIX ONE

# EXTENDING THE EUCHARIST TO THE UNWILLINGLY ABSENT

NOTE: What is suggested here may not be acceptable in certain denominations, due to particular restrictions about who may distribute the Eucharist. In almost all other denominations this proposal will be deemed a novel and possibly controversial idea, despite great precedent for it in the early centuries of the church. Therefore the practice of extending the congregation's Eucharist to those who cannot attend should be undertaken only after careful consideration and planning. Regardless of the outcome of the discussion preceding its use, modification, or even rejection, however, that very discussion will be useful in bringing out theological and pastoral issues that deserve to be studied.

## I. GENERAL INSTRUCTIONS

- The elements from the parish Eucharist may be taken to those who are prevented from attending by virtue of illness, physical inability to come to the place of worship, or a work schedule that regularly prevents attendance.
- A systematic way should be devised of contacting ahead of time those who may wish to have the sacrament brought to them, so that the scheduling can be arranged together with the necessary number of servers.
- The form will vary greatly according to circumstances. This service will necessarily be very brief and confined to only the patient and immediate family members in the case of serious illness. On the other hand, if the impediment to attendance is

related not to serious illness but to immobility or work schedule, a much more ample rite may be followed, with family and other members from the parish taking part. Then the day's lections may be read, hymns sung (particularly if musical accompaniment is available), and other appropriate parts of the day's liturgy employed. What is crucial is that in every instance the service with the unwillingly absent be seen as an extension of the congregation's Eucharist, not as something independent of it.

• The form, therefore, will always vary significantly from a service in which the pastor presides in a home or hospital using bread and wine that were not a part of the parish Eucharist. In the service set forth below, the Eucharistic Prayer is not repeated, but the actions by the congregation at the Table of the Lord will always be recalled.

• It is desirable that the bread and wine be carried to those who are to receive outside of the congregational service as soon thereafter as convenient on that Lord's Day or festival occasion, again so that this service may be seen as an extension of the parish Eucharist. When persons have been absent due to work schedule, however, necessary delay is understandable.

• Those who take communion to others should be carefully selected and trained in this duty.

## II. RITES AT THE CONGREGATION'S EUCHARIST

• At a minimum, at the close of the eucharistic order, the names of those to whom communion is to be taken should be announced, and they should be remembered in prayer. If desired, the names of those who take the sacrament may also be noted. A form such as the following may be used.

> Before we leave the Table of the Lord, we remember those of our congregation who wish to receive communion with us today, but who cannot be present at this place. We share this meal with them and remember them as being part of us. The sacrament will be taken to these, our sisters and brothers:

To Alice Andersen, in the Haven Wood Health Care Center, by John Walters and Helen LaPierre.
To George Figura, in his home, by Anthony Grange and Juan Martinez.
To Anna and Walter Gregory, in their home, by Rita Shaut and Chan Su Kim.
To Alexi Zandi, in Memorial Hospital, by Tanya Brown and Trevor Schmidt.

Before we send forth these servers of the sacrament, let us pray for those to whom they go:

Gracious God, you have bound us together as one congregation among many within your holy church. We remember those who will share with us this day in the feast of grace. According to their particular needs, by the power of your Holy Spirit, minister to Alice, to George, to Anna and Walter, and to Alexi. Strengthen their faith. Enable them to sense our love and concern for them, and give us grace ever to keep them at the center of our care and fellowship; through Jesus Christ, the Host of our Table. Amen.

If the sacramental elements can be conveniently given to the servers directly from the Lord's Table, the servers may go there to receive the bread and wine. Before they depart they may be commissioned with words such as:

Pastor: Go forth in the name of Christ and of this congregation of Christ's people.
Congregation: Depart in peace. Amen.

Those servers whose visits are scheduled immediately after the service may depart during the closing hymn as a reminder of the continuity of their visits with the congregational liturgy.

### III. AT THE PLACE OF THE DISTRIBUTION

One of the servers may say, upon entering the place of distribution:

Christ's peace be in this place. We come as members together with you of *(church name)* to share with you the feast to which our Lord has beckoned all of us.

The service then proceeds as circumstances allow. It is appropriate to read the scriptures used in the congregation, and to join in hymns and prayers from the day's liturgy as the ability of those present warrants. A summary of the sermon may be included.

Before the distribution of the sacrament, the following is said:

Earlier today your brothers and sisters in Christ at *(church name)* gathered at the Table of the Lord. There we offered God our gifts of bread and wine. With God's people across the earth and with the whole company of heaven we proclaimed the holiness of the Lord and recounted the goodness of God to us and to generations before us.

Particularly we remembered our Lord Jesus Christ, how he took bread and wine and gave thanks; how he broke the bread and then delivered the bread and the cup to his disciples. We gave thanks for his whole saving work: his coming in the flesh, his humble ministry of teaching and healing; his death, resurrection, and ascension; his risen presence in the church, made known to us in the breaking of the bread.

We prayed especially that by the power of the Holy Spirit this bread and wine would be for us the body and blood of Christ, that we might more faithfully be Christ's body in the world.

Before we departed from the Table of the Lord in order to share this meal with you, we prayed by name for you, asking God to strengthen you and to bind all of us together in Christ's love.

Now, before receiving this bread and cup, we invite you to pray with us the prayer of the universal church: *(say the Lord's Prayer in unison).*

After the Lord's Prayer, the bread and wine are distributed. Although they have received the sacrament earlier, the servers should again receive in order that this may be a communal meal, shared in fellowship by all believers present. At the distribution these or similar words may be said:

The body of Christ, the bread of heaven. **Amen.**
The blood of Christ, the cup of salvation. **Amen.**

When all have received, a prayer such as this may be used:

Gracious God, you have prepared for us in this life a table around which we may gather as members of your household to know the presence of our risen Lord in the breaking of the bread. This you give us as a sign of your grace, as a foretaste of the great banquet in your eternal kingdom. To that feast of the Lamb you have invited people from east and west, from north and south, that your house may be full. Through this holy sacrament, strengthen us for faithful service in this world and for our pilgrimage to your great banquet hall. Unite us to one another as members of this congregation and to that great company of your saints, which no one can number; through Jesus Christ our Lord. Amen.

At the end of the service, there may be a responsive dismissal, such as:

Let us bless the Lord.
**Thanks be to God.**
The grace of the Lord Jesus Christ, the love of God, and the communion of the Holy Spirit be with us all ever more.
**Amen.**

Remaining eucharistic elements may be returned to the parish church or reverently used according to the practices of the congregation.

# APPENDIX TWO

# THE EUCHARIST IN METHODISM

Because this book is written from an ecumenical perspective, it is appropriate that an appendix be used for elaboration on the eucharistic history, doctrine, and practice of the author's own tradition and that of others within the Wesleyan family of churches.

## THE WESLEYAN BACKGROUND

Around 1733 Wesley wrote for the use of his pupils at Oxford a sermon entitled "The Duty of Constant Communion." In it he urged regular reception—weekly or even daily—and dismantled a host of arguments against such a practice. In 1788, three years before his death, Wesley reissued the sermon with a brief note that he had shortened it a bit because "I then used more words than I do now"; but he added, "I thank God, I have not yet seen cause to alter my sentiments in any point" in that sermon.[1]

This statement by Wesley and the larger understanding it reflected were sources of embarrassment to many nineteenth-century Methodists, who preferred a piety in which sacraments had only a small role. One British Methodist, James H. Rigg, asserted that Wesley had given up sacramental "superstition" in the late 1730s as a result of his Aldersgate experience and hinted darkly that in reissuing the sermon at the age of eighty-five, Wesley was showing signs of senility such that "he was, in different ways, returning in his extreme old age to the love of his youth."[2]

The facts do not bear out the argument. Wesley's consistent attendance at communion strikes us as barely short of overzealous. While evidence can be found in his journal, his diaries are a better guide. For three months, half a year after Aldersgate, we find Wesley receiving communion every Sunday from November 26 through February 25, with the exception of January 7 and February 18 (he had received on the Epiphany, and on February 18 he was guest preacher at a chapel where the Eucharist apparently was not scheduled). But in addition Wesley notes "Communion" in his diary on the following weekdays: November 27; December 21, 22, 23, 24, 26, 27, 28, 29 of 1738; January 1, 6, 13, 15, 16, 25, 26, 27, 31, and February 2, 5, 8, 12, 14, 19, 21, and 23 of 1739. Thus in this three-month period he communicated thirty-eight times. A few instances were occasioned by his administration of the sacrament in an Anglican parish or to sick persons. But in the overwhelming number of instances during this period, Wesley attended a parish church as a member of the congregation. Certainly, then, the Aldersgate experience caused no immediate diminution of eucharist fervor within him; nor can such a lessening be proven by later records (although for many periods the crucial diaries are not available).

Wesley also urged reception on his followers. In a foreshadowing of the vast crowds reported later, on Sunday, February 4, 1739, he made his entry for 10:00 A.M.: "At St. George's, [I] read Prayers [i.e., Anglican Morning Prayer], George Whitfield preached, Communion (one thousand there!)." With respect to the period during which the revival heightened, we are tempted to accuse Wesley of exaggerating attendance figures at preaching services. In 1739, he reported that in aggregate he preached to 14,000 on April 29; to 16,000 on May 13; to 18,500 on May 27; to 19,000 on June 3, and to 22,000 on June 17! The intensity was not maintained, but near the end of this London diary, Wesley reported preaching to 5,000 on May 24, 1741.[3]

Certainly most of the auditors were more curious than convinced by Wesley's preaching; nor can it be expected that all the convinced emulated him in eucharistic piety. Nevertheless, the Methodists were devoted to the sacrament to an extent that caused one recent author to assert: "It is not commonly known today either by Anglicans or by Methodists that the Wesleyan revival was as much a eucharistic revival as an evangelical revival."[4]

While this assertion can be contested in terms of statistics of attendance and frequency, what cannot be debated is the Wesleyan revival of a warm and joyous interpretation of the meaning of the sacrament, as evidenced in the 1745 collection of 166 eucharistic hymns by the Wesley brothers (largely Charles). These hymns combine the objective sacramental character of the Eucharist ("a sure effectual means of grace . . . [that] can never prove of none effect and vain") with subjective apprehension by praying: "Only do thou my heart prepare to find thy Real Presence there, and all thy fulness gain."[5]

The question must be raised, "In 1745 what were Methodists supposed to do with 166 Eucharistic hymns?" Methodism had not yet reached the point of having independent sacramental services; Wesley's followers were instructed to go to the parish church for the Eucharist. But there only the metrical psalms were sung: "newfangled" hymns were characteristic of vile dissenters such as Isaac Watts! Therefore the answer to the question must be: "Methodists were to use these hymns at home for personal preparation prior to receiving communion and for follow-up meditation after reception." Likely they also used them (whether read or sung) within their small groups or bands. Hence these 166 texts at first were primarily for prayer and study. And apparently they were well used. Far from having a limited sale, the 1745 collection went through eleven printings. Most of the Wesleyan eucharistic hymns (whether from the 1745 collection or elsewhere) are not utterly unfamiliar to us. But several that can be readily found warrant comment here for the Wesleyan sacramental theology they reveal.

## WESLEYAN THEOLOGY OF THE EUCHARIST IN SELECTED HYMN TEXTS

Four hymns are explicated here and are printed as edited for *The United Methodist Hymnal*, nos. 613, 616, 635, and 627.[6]

1. O Thou who this mysterious bread
   didst in Emmaus break,
   return herewith our souls to feed,
   and to thy followers speak.

2. Unseal the volume of thy grace,
   apply the gospel word;
   open our eyes to see thy face,
   our hearts to know the Lord.

3. Of thee communing still,
   we mourn till thou the veil remove;
   talk to us, and our hearts shall burn
   with flames of fervent love.

4. Enkindle now the heavenly zeal,
   and make thy mercy known,
   and give our pardoned souls to feel
   that God and love are one.

The poem (no. 29 in the 1745 collection) sets forth the Eucharist as a continuation of the Emmaus meal, not merely as a repetition of what occurred in the upper room prior to the crucifixion. This is, as we have seen, a crucial New Testament insight often lost to the church—after the Wesleys as well as before. At the center of the hymn is the petition, based on Luke 24:35: "Open . . . our hearts to know the Lord." Thus the Eucharist is a continuing means by which Christians recognize the presence of the Risen One in their midst; this reflects the Wesleys' Anglican insistence that the sacrament is an effective means of grace in the present, not simply a subjective pious reflection upon the sacred past. The many allusions to Luke 24:13-35 make this a particularly apt hymn when that pericope is read.

A second hymn was formed from stanzas 1, 4, 14, 22, and 23 of a complex twenty-four stanza poem published in the 1747 collection of *Hymns for Those That Seek and Those That Have Redemption in the Blood of Jesus:*

1. Come, sinners, to the gospel feast,
let every soul be Jesus' guest.
Ye need not one be left behind,
for God hath bid all humankind.

2. Do not begin to make excuse;
ah! do not you his grace refuse;
your worldly cares and pleasures leave,
and take what Jesus hath to give.

3. Come and partake the gospel feast,
be saved from sin, in Jesus rest;
O taste the goodness of our God,
and eat his flesh and drink his blood.

4. See him set forth before your eyes;
behold the bleeding sacrifice;
his offered love make haste to embrace,
and freely now be saved by grace.

5. Ye who believe his record true
shall sup with him and he with you;
come to the feast, be saved from sin,
for Jesus waits to take you in.

In the 1780 *Collection of Hymns for the Use of the People Called Methodists,* the poem had been shortened from twenty-four to nine stanzas. In later hymnals this was reduced further to five stanzas (no. 339 in *UMH*), which deleted all eucharistic allusions and turned the text into an invitation to discipleship but not to communion. With the scraps from the cutting-room floor, the above "new" hymn with a specifically eucharistic focus was constructed for *The United Methodist Hymnal.* The nineteenth-century reduction of Wesley's twenty-four stanzas and the recent reconstruction are rather representative of the decline in eucharistic appreciation after Wesley and of attempts to reverse that decline in our own time.

In the newly edited hymn, believers are urged to set aside all usual excuses (particularly the one that "I, a sinner, am not worthy to receive") and to take what Jesus gives—his sacramental flesh and blood. Through the Eucharist, the Lord offers grace that is not to be refused. The Eucharist sets before us again and again the sacrifice of the cross; here is *anamnesis* in its distinctive and persistant Wesleyan garb, heavily dependent on the theology of the book of Hebrews. But there is also an eschatological motif; the final stanza contains an allusion to the Revelation 3:20. Throughout this recently edited Charles Wesley text echoes the message of John Wesley's sermon "On the Duty of Constant Communion."

The theme of receiving communion in obedience to the command of Jesus is also central to this hymn:

1. Because thou has said:
   "Do this for my sake,"
   the mystical bread
   we gladly partake;
   we thirst for the Spirit
   that flows from above,
   and long to inherit
   thy fullness of love.

2. 'Tis here we look up
   and grasp at thy mind,
   'tis here that we hope
   thine image to find;
   the means of bestowing
   thy gifts we embrace;
   but all things are owing
   to Jesus' grace.

This brief text written in 1748 clearly affirms the Eucharist as a means of grace and a gift of the Spirit through which we find the fullness of divine love. Thus we hope to have within ourselves the mind of Christ, the image of God. In the allusions to Philippians 2:2-5, Genesis 1:26-27, and Colossians 1:15 and 3:10

at the beginning of the second stanza, we glimpse Charles Wesley's ability to exploit his total acquaintance with Scripture in subtle poetic ways.

The final lines stress both the sacramental character of the Eucharist ("the means of bestowing thy gifts we embrace") and the utter dependence of the means of grace on the saving work of Christ ("but all things are owing to Jesus' grace"). Thus Wesley avoids both the reductionism of latter-day Zwinglian memorialist teaching and the distortion the Puritans so rightly feared: a mechanical dispensation of grace detached from Christ's redemptive work and devoid of personal faith.

The most complex of the current Wesleyan eucharistic texts is "O the depth of love divine" (no. 57 in the 1745 collection):

1. O the depth of love divine,
   the unfathomable grace!
   Who shall say how bread and wine
   God into us conveys!
   How the bread his flesh imparts,
   how the wine transmits his blood,
   fills his faithful people's hearts
   with all the life of God!

2. Let the wisest moral show
   how we the grace receive;
   feeble elements bestow
   a power not theirs to give.
   Who explains the wondrous way,
   how through these the virtue came?
   These the virtue did convey,
   yet still remain the same.

3. How can spirits heavenward rise,
   by earthly matter fed,
   drink herewith divine supplies
   and eat immortal bread?
   Ask the Father's Wisdom how:
   Christ who did the means ordain;

angels round our altars bow
to search it out, in vain.

4. Sure and real is the grace,
the manner be unknown;
only meet us in thy ways
and perfect us in one.
Let us taste the heavenly powers,
Lord, we ask for nothing more.
Thine to bless, 'tis only ours
to wonder and adore.[7]

Anglicanism combined Lutheran and Calvinian interpretations of the Eucharist, and this text is an exposition of Calvin's sacramental theology.[8] The opening line aside, Wesley seems to be with Zwingli through the third line of the second stanza; the Zurich reformer rejected any particular manifestation of Christ in the Supper because he could not explain how that epiphany could occur. So also Wesley asserts that not even the wisest person can explain how bread and wine can be more than bread and wine; they are feeble elements that presumably can bestow nothing other than physical nutrition.

But in the final section of stanza 2 Wesley turns the skeptical questions of the Zwinglians aside: Bread and wine did convey a power they do not have in themselves. *(Virtue,* from the Latin root *virtus,* means "power" in this case, not moral rectitude; recall that Calvin's eucharistic theology is called "virtualism," since he attributed the eucharistic presence of Christ to the mysterious power of the Spirit. The final lines of stanza 2 are in the past tense—apparently because this was a text Methodists were to meditate on after having experienced Christ's power in the sacrament. Hence this hymn is best sung at the close of the eucharistic service.)

Stanza 3 begins with another set of Zwinglian-like questions. Calvin rejected the notion that somehow Christ comes down to the altar in the sacrament, replacing this with the suggestion that at the Eucharist we are taken upward to join the heavenly Christ. Zwinglians find this nonsensical and ask how our spirits can rise to heaven, and how while bound to earth we eat and drink what is divine and immortal.

Wesley answers with sophisticated theological humor bordering on sarcasm. If you would know "how," says Wesley, ask Jesus Christ—the one who ordained the means of grace by the command "Do this." ("Father's Wisdom" is a title for Christ, based on the Pauline appellation of 1 Corinthians 1:24, "Christ the power of God and the wisdom of God.") Then comes the humor: You can ask Christ how all this can be, but you could not understand even if you were told. For the very angels of heaven hover above our altars in stunned reverence, unable to grasp the great mystery. Here one catches the unmistakable echoes of Calvin's assertion: "Now, if anyone should ask me how this takes place, I shall not be ashamed to confess that it is a secret too lofty for either my mind to comprehend or my words to declare. And to speak more plainly, I rather experience than understand it."[9]

This assertion of Calvin is expanded in Wesley's final stanza. The reality of the Eucharist as a reliable means of grace is affirmed, but the manner in which this occurs is to remain unknown. It is a divinely chosen way, which creates communion between God and the church; hence we are to observe it. We ask to taste the heavenly powers of the sacramental bread and wine, not to understand them. God's gift is to bless us. Our response is not to ask questions but to bow in wonder and adoration.

For both Calvinists and Wesleyans, this may well be the finest doctrinal (as distinct from devotional) eucharistic hymn in English. In any case, both groups, having been widely influenced by Zwinglians and other rationalists, would do well to recover this hymn for their contemporary instruction in our historical roots.

## METHODIST PRACTICE

Methodist eucharistic practices are far too divergent for detailed comment. Only three issues can be touched upon briefly.

(1) Methodists are justified in boasting of an "open communion table" in the sense that we welcome communicants of all denominations and do not exclude those who have been baptized but not yet confirmed. (Indeed, children have usually been welcomed at Methodist Tables as soon as they could grasp the elements.) But sometimes "open" has been construed in such a way as to make the eucharistic hour indistinguishable from the congregation's coffee hour.

Historically Methodists did not blush to hold certain exclusionary standards. Unlike their contemporaries, especially the Puritans, the early Methodists did not require of prospective communicants any absolute outward evidence of conversion or an unassailable conviction of assurance. Wesley's view that the Eucharist could be a "converting ordinance" allowed that changed lives and confident profession of faith could come *through* the eucharistic means of grace. Still, sincerity and earnestness in the seeker were tested in various ways. As early as 1747, admission to Methodist communions was by ticket or token, evidence that those who came were participating in the society meetings in good faith; and in early American Methodism slave-holders could be barred from communion.

As to the usual assumption that communion is for the baptized, certainly Wesley could assume that Anglicans joining his renewal society had indeed been baptized. In our day, practice concerning communion of the unbaptized does well to adhere to the counsel of Geoffrey Wainwright:

> *No one should be refused communion who has been moved by the celebration of the sign then in progress to seek saving fellowship with the Lord through eating the bread and drinking the wine.*
>
> But then he should be brought to *baptism*, and *soon*. For if he has on this first and exceptional occasion been drawn to the Lord's table as the recipient of a salvation to which he was hitherto a stranger, he has by the very reception of salvation been constituted a witness to the saving work of God. . . . A man who then refuses baptism is not in earnest about his desire to enter the kingdom, and he will not be admitted to the Lord's table again

> until he has been so persuaded. (Italics and masculine language are Wainwright's)[10]

It should be added that those who consistently wish to receive the Eucharist without having been baptized likely suffer from a significant misunderstanding about the meaning of one or both of the sacraments.

(2) Another issue concerns the familiar Methodist pattern of quarterly communion. This has nothing to do with the quarterly schedule instituted by Zwingli, even though those who want the sacrament no more often frequently share the theological assumptions of the Swiss reformer. Rather, quarterly communion among Methodists is a remnant of Wesley's insistence that only the ordained may administer the sacrament.

In early American Methodism, most preachers were laity, specially licensed to this ministry. The fully ordained, very few in number, were given governmental jurisdiction over wide geographical areas and were directed to visit each location four times a year. Thus these "presiding elders" (later known as "district superintendents") conducted the business of the congregations in sessions called "quarterly conferences"; they also administered Baptism and the Lord's Supper on these visits. Because of the power of ecclesiastical inertia, many congregations continued quarterly communion long after they had ordained clergy appointed to them as pastors—even though in his 1784 instructions to the American church Wesley advised "the [ordained] elders to administer the Supper of the Lord on every Lord's Day."[11]

(3) Finally, the use of wine among Methodists deserves brief consideration for the sake of historical accuracy. Wesley did not object to the use of wine either for personal or sacramental reasons. (He did, however, distinguish between wine and distilled spirits; the latter were to be avoided, as was all drunkenness.) On an occasion when thousands attended one Methodist Eucharist, it was reported rather wittily that they "slipped away" thirty-five bottles of wine.[12] Thus Methodist prohibitions against sacramental wine are rooted in a later

abstinence movement, not in Wesleyan precedent. The use of unfermented grape juice was indeed an impossibility until the process preventing fermentation was perfected in the nineteenth century. Contemporary debates about wine versus grape juice will not be solved on the basis of these historical facts, however, but must be worked through in ways suggested in the body of this book.

For scholarly discussions of the Eucharist in Wesleyanism, see:

Borgen, Ole E. *John Wesley on the Sacraments.* Nashville: Abingdon Press, 1972.

Bowmer, John C. *The Lord's Supper in Methodism, 1791–1960.* London: Epworth Press, 1961.

Parris, John R. *John Wesley's Doctrine of the Sacraments.* London: Epworth Press, 1963.

Sanders, Paul S. "An Appraisal of John Wesley's Sacramentalism in the Evolution of Early American Methodism." Unpublished Ph.D. dissertation, Union Theological Seminary, New York, 1954.

Staples, Rob L. *Outward Sign and Inward Grace: The Place of Sacraments in Wesleyan Spirituality.* Kansas City: Beacon Hill Press, 1991.

# NOTES

## PROLOGUE

1. The terms *Eucharist, Mass, Supper of the Lord,* and *Holy Communion* all refer to the same service of Christian worship, but each carries in its name a differing shade of meaning; these names, when taken together, are complementary.

*Eucharist* is the oldest term and one that has become increasingly popular in our time after centuries of neglect. It is formed from two ancient Greek roots: *eu,* a prefix meaning "good" or "well," and *charis,* meaning "gift" or "grace." (The second root is the basis for the English terms *charisma* and *charismatic,* as well as being the crucial New Testament term regularly translated as "grace.") Usually *Eucharist* is rendered into English as "thanksgiving"—it is the gratitude we express for all good gifts, which come from God—and the meal is itself a means of grace given to the church by Jesus Christ. The disadvantage posed by the unfamiliarity of the term is more than offset by its positive connotations; these helpfully counterbalance popular notions that the sacrament is a dreary or even morbid recollection of the passion of Jesus rather than an experience of the presence of the risen Christ. Because its history goes back so far (indeed into the New Testament period itself) the term can be well-accepted across denominational barriers by Orthodox, Catholic, and Protestant Christians. The other three titles are more denominationally oriented.

*Mass,* the term most familiar to Roman Catholics in the English-speaking world, probably results from the final words of the eucharistic liturgy in the Middle Ages. At the end of the service, the priest dismissed the people with the Latin formula, "*Ite, missa est.*" (Freely rendered this means, "Go now; you are dismissed.") The word *missa* came to be applied to the very book from which the priest read the entire rite: the Missal. And in an altered form it came to be a generic term for the whole service: the Mass. Thus today it means that particular form of eucharistic liturgy used by Roman Catholics (or certain Anglo-Catholics within the Anglican churches). Because it is so specific, it is the least useful of the four common titles for the church's feast; while not anti-ecumenical, it is far less ecumenically helpful than *Eucharist.*

*The Supper of the Lord* or *the Lord's Supper* are terms popularized by the Protestant Reformers who wished to emphasize their objections to certain beliefs and practices that were conveyed by the term *Mass.* The advantage of these terms is that they clearly convey the idea of a meal (which none of the other three designations does). The titles are used especially by Presbyterians, Baptists, and those of kindred theological traditions; sometimes the designations are reduced simply to the term *the Supper.*

One difficulty is that *the Lord's Supper* is too readily equated with *the Last Supper,* so that sacramental joy and effectiveness in the present tend to get lost in subjective meditation on the event that occurred in the upper room on the night of Jesus' betrayal and arrest. The problem has been compounded by some liturgies in the Reformation tradition, which have obscured the holy meal as a feast with the risen Lord in favor of just such concentration on the events of Holy Thursday and Good Friday; this has isolated the sacrament both from Jesus' meals with his followers during his teaching ministry and from the post-resurrection meals reported in the Gospels of Mark (16:14), Luke (24:30-35 and 41-43) and John (21:9-14).

*Holy Communion* is a title particularly popular among Anglicans, Methodists, and Lutherans. *Communion* connotes communication or sharing both between God and the people, and among the members within the worshiping community. *Holy* implies that whatever such experiences may be had in other ways, the meal is a unique and divinely appointed means through which Christians engage one another and together are in communion with God. *Communion* is used in a related way in many English translations of 1 Corinthians 10:16 ("communion of the body of Christ, communion of the blood of Christ"); in ways unrelated to the liturgical meal, the term is also used in renderings of 2 Corinthians 6:14 and 13:13.

One point of potential confusion: While the word *communion* alone often is used generically to refer to the sacrament, that word also has a very specific use when talking about the sacramental liturgy; the "communion" refers to the actual reception of the bread and the cup, as distinct from the other central eucharistic acts of "offering" (the bringing to the table of the bread and wine, and their acceptance by the presider); "thanksgiving" (the great prayer over the bread and wine); and "fraction" (the breaking of the loaf into pieces prior to its distribution to the people). This presents an ecumenical difficulty. Those who normally use the phrase "Holy Communion" often understand *communion* to mean the entire rite. Those who do not usually refer to the entire service as "Holy Communion" (such as Roman Catholics) regularly use *communion* to mean the time of actual distribution only.

While not inherent in the title itself, the words *Holy Communion* often bring with them meanings that are unduly individualistic and introspective. So it is not surprising that traditions that have used these words for centuries are very open to reintroducing (instead or in addition) the ancient word *Eucharist.*

## 1. CENTRAL MEANINGS BEHIND THE MEAL

1. The Latin *panis* is clearly preserved in our term *pancake*—literally, "a bread cake"—and in the baking vessel called simply a "pan." ("With" in Latin is *con,* but for ease in pronunciation, an *n* commonly becomes an *m* when preceding *p*.)

2. Throughout this book, the terms *bread* and *wine* will be used generically. Some will think of communion bread as something very unlike anything usually consumed at a table, even as others will think of drinking grape juice rather than fermented wine. The problem of using alcoholic wine is considered in chapter 7; use of the term *wine* throughout the book is not intended to foreclose that discussion, which has important pastoral implications as well as a complex historical background.

3. Some readers will recognize that these are the categories under which I examined the sacrament of Christian initiation in *Baptism: Christ's Act in the Church* (Nashville: Abingdon Press, 1982). The similarity is more than a matter of literary convenience. Baptism and Eucharist are linked by the completeness with which they proclaim the story of God's work in our midst.

In reaction to the medieval system of seven sacraments, the Protestant Reformers insisted that only two rites are sacraments, even while retaining the other five (confirmation, penance, marriage, ordination, extreme unction) in some form. The Reformers argued for this distinction primarily on the basis that Jesus clearly "instituted" or "ordered" the first two rites, while the other five were based more on pastoral experience and the weight of tradition than on the clear commandment of the Lord Jesus (known technically as "dominical warrant"). This argument does not endure well given the things we have learned since the Reformation about the historical ministry of Jesus of Nazareth, the formation of the New Testament, or later tradition and doctrinal development. Thus in our day the issue of how many things should be called sacraments may need to be reopened. See, for example, the case for all seven in James F. White, *Sacraments as God's Self-Giving* (Nashville: Abingdon Press, 1983).

Even so, White's distinction between Baptism and Eucharist, on the one hand, and the five "apostolic and natural sacraments," on the other, suggests that the Reformers may have been on to something, if for the wrong reason. Baptism and Eucharist have a theological priority over the other rites of the church; even if necessary and revelatory, all other rites tell the story of creation, covenant, Christ, church, and coming kingdom less amply.

4. See particularly Romans 8:18-25.

5. The arrangement of the various portions of scripture within the Christian canon should not be taken as accidental. The first three chapters of Genesis and the last two chapters of the Revelation have a crucial complementarity; they are the "great bookends" of the biblical story. The destruction of the sea in Revelation 21:1 goes unnoticed or unappreciated until it is recalled that in Genesis 1 the sea is the symbol of chaos. Until the end of time God restrains that chaos and sets its boundaries, but at the end the chaos is utterly vanquished. In Genesis, God creates light on the first day—independent of the creation of sun and moon as sources of light, the latter not created until day four. Revelation 21:23 asserts that the heavenly city "has no need of sun or moon to shine on it, for the glory of God is its light, and its lamp is the Lamb." In Genesis 3 there is a garden with rivers and trees of critical importance; therein live all the dwellers of earth (albeit only two). In Revelation 22 there is a city for all the inhabitants, again with a river and a crucial kind of tree.

6. God, challenging Job, asserts a divine magnanimity unrecognized by self-centered humanity:

> "Who has cut a channel for the torrents of rain,
> and a way for the thunderbolt,
> to bring rain on a land where no one lives,
> on the desert, which is empty of human life,
> to satisfy the waste and desolate land,
> and to make the ground put forth grass?"
> (Job 38:25-27)

And the book of Jonah, in its final words, stresses that God has a delightful regard for the city of Nineveh not only because of its 120,000 human inhabitants but also because of its "many animals" (Jonah 4:11).

In short, a thoroughly biblical view sees creation as God's sharing of self not only with humanity, but also with animals and plants and the very soil. The two passages just cited, while canonically remote from Genesis, challenge our glib assumption that Genesis 1:28 gives humanity an imperialistic authority over all else. But human kinship with the animals and with the soil is indeed implied in Genesis 1–2, taken as a whole, and God's use of the soil to form humanity is an important theological affirmation of the interdependency of the earth and us humans who live on it. The frequent exegetical isolation of 1:28 is an example of disregarding context in order to have a pretext for doing what we want to do, or a justification for what we have already done.

7. *The Book of Common Prayer* of The Episcopal Church (New York: Church Hymnal Corporation, 1977), 372 (Rite II, Prayer C).

8. While the put-down of Jesus as a glutton and drunkard may to some extent reflect his attendance at feasts and parties, in a way obscure to those of us who are not sufficiently familiar with Torah, it more likely was a deliberate allusion to Deuteronomy 21:18-21:

> If someone has a stubborn and rebellious son who will not obey his father and mother, who does not heed them when they discipline him, then his father and his mother shall take hold of him and bring him out to the elders of his town at the gate of that place. They shall say to the elders of his town, "This son of ours is stubborn and rebellious. He will not obey us. He is a glutton and a drunkard." Then all the men of the town shall stone him to death. So you shall purge the evil from your midst.

Thus the real charge was not that Jesus overate or drank but that he was a stubborn rebel and thus should be put to death as a way of purging evil from the community.

9. This "reading backward" is most evident in the Gospel reports that Jesus instructed his followers again and again to "tell no one" (e.g.,

Matthew 8:4; Mark 5:43; 7:36; 9:9; and applicable parallels throughout). This is very strange if the goal of the Christian faith is to "go into all the world and tell everyone," as the concluding chapters of the Synoptics assert. The apparent discrepancy is resolved in passages such as Matthew 17:9, in which silence is commanded until "after the resurrection." The theological point is this: Except when read in the light of the end of the story, the deeds of Jesus would incorrectly identify him as a worker of wonders, a kind of religious magician with which the world of his day abounded. Only after the resurrection can his mighty acts be seen as signs of the new creation that he has come to inaugurate; only after the resurrection can his followers have appropriate, rather than misguided, faith.

## 2. KEY BIBLICAL UNDERSTANDINGS OF THE EUCHARIST

1. The Hebrew term to which *anamnesis* corresponds is *ZKR (zeker).*

2. Our tendency to settle for *within* (when *among* is better) stems in part at least from an ambiguity in the Greek of certain New Testament passages. When Jesus says, for example, "The kingdom of God is ——— you" (Luke 17:21), the Greek preposition *entos* can be translated either "among" or "within." The former is used without qualification by The Jerusalem Bible. The Revised Standard Version and The New English Bible together with their successors, the New Revised Standard Version and The Revised English Bible, all qualify their translation "among" ("in the midst of" in the RSV) with footnotes that allow "within" as an alternative. The King James Version uses "within," as does the New International Version, though the latter notes "among" as an alternative. While the rendering of Luke 17:21 is a complicated and technical matter, the discussion surrounding it represents something much broader: The tendency of recent Christian piety to be individualistic and subjective, whereas Jewish and early Christian piety was more corporate and objective. These contrasting tendencies often are found in very exaggerated form in eucharistic practice and devotion.

3. The categories should not be maintained rigidly. For many, the sermon is not heard at all but is seen, since they receive what is preached by way of sign language or lip reading. Even for those with no hearing loss, what a preacher does that can be seen communicates much, either positively or negatively (as anyone knows who has watched some speaker's graceful or clumsy use of gesture). Conversely,

sacramental celebration makes ample use of words. In some rare instances persons have tried eucharistic celebrations with gestures alone; to the extent that these have been authentic communications, it is because rites with words were thoroughly familiar to the worshipers. A celebrant who speaks only English may without words be able to communicate the eucharistic experience to a Christian congregation that speaks French only. But it is not likely that a group of people who have never heard of Jesus Christ could adequately grasp the gospel story told in the Eucharist through nonverbal clues alone.

4. The analogy of liturgy to drama often brings with it comments by Søren Kierkegaard (*Purity of Heart* [New York: Harper and Bros., 1938], Part XII) that are at once insightful and misleading. The Danish theologian complained that too often Christian congregations see themselves as audiences to be entertained by the preacher. Kierkegaard rightly insisted that the worshipers are also "on stage" and should see themselves as actors totally involved in the liturgical event. The preacher is, in effect, the prompter who helps the actors with their lines. So far, so good. But then Kierkegaard made, in my opinion, a fatal mistake by suggesting that the audience is God. His analogy tends both to make God passive and to turn grace into good works. (Presumably we on stage have to do a superb job, or divine applause will not be forthcoming.)

Thus the Kierkegaardian analogy needs to be extended. God is at once the playwright, producer, and director. God is intimately involved at every phase of the drama. The audience is not God but the world, for in part, at least, worship is a form of testimony from the church to the world. It may be that even for the finest performance, the audience will decide to stay at home, but heaven help the church if the world stays away because, despite the best efforts of the playwright/producer/director, we actors make the divine drama seem hopelessly dull!

5. Gregory Dix, *The Shape of the Liturgy* (London: Dacre Press, 1945), 56. Particularly note this comment: "If the command 'Do this' does not mean that our Lord supposed He was instituting a new rite, what does it mean? The emphasis must be on the other half of the sentence—'for the re-calling of Me.' He is not instituting a new custom, but investing a universal Jewish custom with *a new and peculiar meaning*."

6. Many volumes have been written in debate over whether : (a) Jesus' last meal with his disciples was an actual Passover meal, as the chronologies of the Synoptics suggest; (b) the Passover meal actually

occurred on the evening following Jesus' crucifixion, as John's Gospel clearly implies; and even Luke 22:15 can be interpreted to mean that Jesus' desire to eat the Passover was not fulfilled but frustrated by his early death; (c) the whole historical issue is beside the point, assuming that all such accounts are a reinterpretation of Jesus' ministry in the light of the cross or a pious (though not necessarily illegitimate) fabrication by early Christians who were seeking to understand why eating and drinking together held such power for them. If (b) rather than (a) is true, then what kind of meal was it in the upper room? A weekly sabbath meal? Some special pre-Passover meal? A fellowship meal such as was common in the culture between a rabbi and his disciples? Entrance into that convoluted and highly technical debate is beyond the scope of this book. It is sufficient here to affirm two things: Wherever the roots of the church's Eucharist may lie, (a) within the first century it became a weekly act of the church and (b) at the same time bore symbolic connotations of a second Exodus, of which Christ is both the true Paschal Lamb offered up for the people and the new Moses who leads God's people with liberating power into a new covenant.

7. See Vernard Ellar's exposition of the last two chapters of the book of Revelation in *The Most Revealing Book of the Bible: Making Sense Out of Revelation* (Grand Rapids: William B. Eerdmans, 1974), 193-212.

## 3. FAITH SEEKING UNDERSTANDING

1. I am deliberately avoiding too heavy a reliance on certain classical terms that can today lead to great confusion. For example, the term *real* is often used in connection with the particular thing (*res*), while *idealism* is used to speak of the "ideas" or "forms" of Platonism. But two problems present themselves immediately. First, in the history of philosophy, *realism* and *idealism* are precise terms, and their technical meaning can change from one system of thought to another. Second, popular use of these terms often fails to conform to any of the technical definitions, which only confuses the matter further.

This is especially the case with the often-used phrase "Real Presence" (of Christ in the Eucharist). On the level of popular understanding the term seems to mean simply that a true presence of Christ, however defined, is being affirmed. But in the history of doctrine, *real* is closely related to (and derived from) the Latin *res*. Hence at a technical level

"Real Presence" can imply a divine epiphany very specifically attached to the "thing"—that is, the bread and wine. Then we are in quite a different ballpark, as will be evident as this chapter proceeds to wrestle with the complexities of the Extreme Realism of the Platonists and the Moderate Realism of the Aristotelians. Since almost no one today operates in either of these philosophical systems, the term "Real Presence" engenders more confusion than clarity in the contemporary church. Hence I choose not to use the term, though I strongly affirm that experience of Christ in our midst to which it seeks to point.

2. All three options were suggested by some medieval theologians (Peter of Capua, for example) as possible modes of transubstantiation. Ultimately the third possibility drove out the other two, but there is a dispute as to the time at which the third option came to be the only acceptable definition of "transubstantiation."

Usually it has been assumed that in promulgating the formal doctrine of transubstantiation in 1215, the Fourth Lateran Council intended the third option only. But some scholars have argued that Lateran IV was not clear on this, and may have regarded the term *transubstantiation* generically—and thus applicable to more than the last of the three possibilities. However that may be, two things are clear: (1) Although Radbertus of Corbie, France, is credited with originating (in 831) the idea of a transformation in the substances of bread and wine, the word *transubstantiation* itself was not introduced until the twelfth century. (2) When Thomas Aquinas set forth the definitive teaching on transubstantiation in the mid-thirteenth century (shortly after Lateran IV), it was the third option that he accepted to the exclusion of the others. His position was absolutized by the Council of Trent, which may or may not have gone beyond Lateran IV in this regard.

3. Because the Latin prefix *con* means "with," thereby calling to mind the Lutheran formula "in, with, and under," the Lutheran understanding of eucharistic Presence has often been called "consubstantiation." The term can be attractive for two reasons: (1) It clearly distinguishes the Lutheran teaching from "transubstantiation" and (2) yet implies that the reformed theology has solid historic continuity. (In our own day, Roman Catholic theologians who wish to back away from a belief in substance while affirming a continuity with the tradition have similarly altered the term *transubstantiation*—in this era by devising related words such as *transsignification* and *transtemporalization.*)

But *consubstantiation* is an imprecise term for the Lutheran position.

First, it can be used for a much more restricted purpose in discussing one particular medieval way of looking at Aristotelian eucharistic doctrine long before the time of Luther. To use the same term for two quite different developments in widely separated historical periods only creates confusion. Second, Luther was a Nominalist who presumably did not believe in substance as separate from accidents at all—as certainly his adherents today do not. Whatever polemical value the term *consubstantiation* may have had for Lutherans in the past, its use is now best avoided.

4. To say that *anamnesis* in the Hebraic sense slipped from consciousness is simply to say that its formal meaning was obscured, so that theologians interpreted it as "remembrance" in a Western, intellectualized sense. But this is not to suggest that the church thereby lost the reality of experiencing the past—or the future—by enacting it in the present. Even when the technical meaning of *anamnesis* was forgotten, anamnetic experience was frequently attested in hymnody, preaching, and architecture. And *anamensis,* even if unrecognized and distorted, surely underlay the medieval notion that the Mass represented Calvary so completely that the eucharistic rite could effect an atoning sacrifice for actual sin. Even in Calvin's notion that at the Eucharist the faithful are carried into heaven by the Spirit, there is more than a remnant of Hebraic *anamnesis* in its forward dimension. We can "remember" the future as well as the past—though likely Calvin had no awareness of this connection to Hebraic understanding.

Thus in various ways across the centuries the experiential reality of *anamnesis* was preserved, though the conscious awareness of it was lost until our own century, when Johannes Pedersen wrote his study *Israel I-II* (published in Danish in 1920 and in English in 1926 [London: Oxford University Press]).

5. From Calvin's *Form of Church Prayers,* Geneva, 1542; English translation of R. C. D. Jasper and G. J. Cuming, *Prayers of the Eucharist: Early and Reformed,* 2nd ed. (New York: Oxford University Press, 1980), 156.

6. The notion that the sacraments are effective simply by being observed is encapsuled in the traditional formula *ex opere operato*—literally, "from the work done." That is, the "validity" of the Eucharist does not depend on the moral character of the priest, nor on the faith of the recipient, so long as the recipient erects no barrier to the grace offered. In contrast is the formula *ex opere operans* (or *ex opere operantis*), which implies that the sacrament does depend on the faith of the priest or of

the recipient in order to work. The Council of Trent, judging that at least some Reformation teaching fell into this error of subjectivism, officially adopted a position of *ex opere operato,* often also called *opus operatum.* The difference between these viewpoints is often the subject of stereotyping; there is oversimplification both in the Protestant polemic that Trent embraced a magical sacramental view and in Trent's perception that Protestantism rejected outright the historic principle that the sacraments communicate the grace they signify.

7. John Calvin, *Institutes of the Christian Religion,* IV.XVII.33; IV.XVII.7.

## 4. FROM AGE TO AGE

1. Contemporary translations of the sources are readily available with commentary in Bard Thompson's *Liturgies of the Western Church* (New York: World Publishing Co., 1961) and without commentary in *Prayers of the Eucharist: Early and Reformed,* by R. C. D. Jasper and G. J. Cuming, 2nd ed. (New York: Oxford University Press, 1980).

2. Though he came to be canonized a saint after his martyrdom, for much of his ministry Hippolytus was regarded as a schismatic, holding to opinions and practices that had gone out of fashion. In what seems to be an oxymoron, the Roman Catholic Church regards him as "St. Hippolytus, Anti-Pope to Popes Callistus I, Urban I, and Pontianus."

3. It is sometimes lamented that we have from the New Testament itself no clear and complete liturgical data. The fact that the earliest Christians worshiped is evident, but exactly what form their worship took is not reported. While the New Testament has imbedded in it fragments of what earlier were hymns, prayers, creedal statements, and homiletical material, these have been woven into a tapestry that disguises their original appearance.

Far from being lamentable, all of this may well be within the providence of God. Had the New Testament reported the original liturgical forms and practices too precisely, this would have encouraged a liturgical fundamentalism that could shortly have stifled and then destroyed vital worship. Liturgical content always must be grounded in and centered on the core of Christian faith, but in order truly to be the work of the people, the forms and practices must be adapted to each particular culture and age. The silence of the New Testament leaves room precisely for that.

4. The primary reason for dismissing the unbaptized was theologi-

cal, having to do with the church as a community of the committed, bound together by initiation into Christ's death and resurrection. But in the era of persecution, the dismissal of the unbaptized served a secondary purpose related to security concerns and threat of martyrdom.

Since the Romans were strict about legal rights and would not resort to hearsay as a basis for punishment, there had to be an objective way of identifying those to be exterminated because of adherence to the Christian faith. Baptism was a very objective test; once baptized, you were a prime candidate for martyrdom.

Always there must have been the possibility that among the catechumens in a worship service there might be government informers, seeking to establish the names of the baptized. In particular, the baptized who were absent due to infirmity needed to be protected from extermination and the fear of it; yet their names would be mentioned in the intercessions. So it was good that before the intercessions the unbaptized would be dismissed, even if for reasons basically theological. Then the doors were locked—not because the rites were clandestine, but because no one must be allowed to learn the identity of the baptized communicants present or those absent for good cause who were remembered in the prayers. To this day, after the "Liturgy of the Catechumens" in the services of the Orthodox churches, a deacon cries out, "The doors! The doors!"—a vestige of the time when a doorkeeper needed to be reminded that the entrance to the building was now to be locked and guarded.

Similar concerns may help to account for the reason why infants were baptized in some periods (as both Hippolytus and Tertullian reported) and yet denied baptism in other eras up to the time of Constantine. Then, persecution past, infants could be baptized without the fear that their initiation would mark them as enemies of the emperor.

5. Some clergy were illiterate and recited the liturgy from memory. Even so, the widespread Protestant view that learning almost totally died out in the church during the Middle Ages is plainly inaccurate. The monastic communities were centers of scholarship, with libraries containing vast stores of classical treasures; it was from this base that the university system arose in Europe. Education among laity was another matter, and often even nobility were illiterate.

The form of eucharistic rite I am discussing in this section is the Low Mass on a nonfestival Sunday. For a happier view of the period, see the description of High Mass on Pentecost in *At All Times and in All Places* by Massey H. Shepherd, Jr. (New York: The Seabury Press, 1965), 35-47.

6. Reasons for the change can be debated. Certainly many altars, particularly in pilgrimage churches, came to have sacred relics displayed above them, such that a priest could not see over the top. But this could be a result of an earlier emphasis on mystery, which discouraged the congregation from observing too closely the action at the altar. Even in earlier times, draperies were hung around the altar; during the central action of the Eucharist these were drawn shut so that, being unable to view the action, the people would sense the wonder of the unknown.

In the Orthodox churches the curtains evolved into a solid screen bearing icons (the *iconostasis*), pierced only by "the royal doors," which were themselves closed during the *anaphora*. Only recently have some Orthodox congregations chosen to leave the royal doors open throughout the service. Many medieval churches in Catholic Europe had chancel screens or even walls, but their origins may have had less to do with mystery than with more practical motives—such as separating the space between the monastic community and the townspeople, or even controlling drafts.

7. The Fourth Lateran Council in 1215 made the reception of communion at Easter an obligation for all the faithful. From the necessity for such legislation, we can infer that even many Christians who attended Mass with some regularity were declining to receive communion for years on end.

8. Bibles were scarce, and education in matters such as exegetical and homiletical training for clergy were yet more rare in the Middle Ages. Even literate parish priests could not be expected to preach regularly. The task, therefore, was taken up by monastic orders devoted to this ministry. The Dominicans were designated by the abbreviation "O.P." Both in English and Latin these letters stand for "Order of Preachers" (*Ordo Praedicatorum*), for the Dominicans were originally itinerant preachers. They—together with the Franciscans, Benedictines, and other orders—supplied the church with many of its preachers.

Sermons were delivered primarily at times separate from the Mass, such as Sunday afternoons or weekday evenings. This accounts for the fact that in a typical medieval church the pulpit may be far from the high altar, often attached to a pier halfway down the nave, around which the listeners gathered at sermon time. In good weather, preaching often was done out of doors. Temporary wooden pulpits erected for an occasional preaching mission by an itinerant friar evolved into permanent pulpits attached to the exterior of the building or located nearby. Medieval preaching often was done in the context of a simple liturgy of prayer and praise ("prone"), which later became a model for Protestant preaching services, particularly under Zwingli.

9. Protestant writers customarily assert that the medieval church "withheld the cup from the laity." While accurate, the statement is incomplete. In fact, in cases where other clergy were present as communicants, the officiating priest alone drank from the chalice, due to the possibility of spilling the contents when transmitting the cup from person to person. But even if the withholding of the cup had some practical purpose, the fact that the laity (unlike the clergy) never received the wine represents a discrimination against the laity, which had many other manifestations as well.

Theologians quickly devised elaborate philosophical arguments to show that the full substance of both Christ's body and blood is contained in the bread alone and in the wine alone. Thus to receive either element without the other is to be deprived of nothing, for the whole divine gift is in each in entirety. This argument Luther derided strongly and sarcastically in his 1520 treatise *The Babylonian Captivity of the Church.*

10. The Reformers could be quite intemperate. They consistently derided the medieval silent Mass (which one attended primarily in order to "see the miracle") as "the dumb show," and called anointing oil "the pope's grease." The early litany of the Anglican Church prayed to be delivered "from the tyranny of the bishop of Rome and all his detestable enormities." Some statements were more moderate in tone. But when Article XXV of The Thirty-Nine Articles of Religion of the Church of England asserted that "the Sacraments were not ordained of Christ to be gazed upon or carried about," condemnation was clearly intended of the practices of the exposition and benediction of the blessed sacrament, and processions with the monstrance on feasts such as Corpus Christi.

11. As impractical as this idea of conducting worship in four tongues seems to us, it had a practical concern growing out of Luther's knowledge of earlier reform movements. He noted his desire to train those "who could also be of service to Christ in foreign lands and able to converse with the natives there, in order to avoid the experience of the Waldensians in Bohemia, who confined their faith to one language so completely, that they cannot speak correctly and intelligently with anyone [who does not] first learn their language." Then, alluding to

Acts 2, Luther added with characteristically wry humor: "This was not the method of the Holy Spirit at the beginning. He did not tarry until all the world came to Jerusalem and studied Hebrew" (Preface to *Deutsche Messe* of 1526, *Works of Martin Luther,* vol. VI [Philadelphia: Muhlenberg Press, 1932], 172. Those whom Luther calls "the Waldensians in Bohemia" are known more correctly as the Hussites or Bohemian Brethren; the Waldensians were located in Italy, but apparently the followers of Hus received episcopal ordination from these Waldensians, hence the confusion of terms.)

12. Zwingli's preaching order was simple, but it retained some surprising elements, including intercessions for the dead and the *Ave Maria* (spoken). The eucharistic order was more elaborate, prescribing use of Epistle and Gospel (after which the lector kissed the book), the *Gloria in Excelsis* and Apostles' Creed, and Psalm 113:1-9 (all arranged for responsive recitation between men and women). For the full 1525 orders, see Bard Thompson, *Liturgies of the Western Church,* 147-56; or for a skeletal outline with only the text of the eucharistic action itself given, see Jasper and Cuming, *Prayers of the Eucharist,* 134-35.

Luther despaired of the Anabaptist contention that the work of the Spirit is so exclusively within the believers as to be thwarted by any outward form (and particularly by prescribed liturgies). In a famous quip, Luther suggested that one of their leaders, Thomas Müntzer, had "swallowed the Holy Ghost, feathers and all" (cited without further attribution in Thompson, *Liturgies of the Western Church,* 97).

13. I speak as a chastened transgressor, having often uttered such commentaries and produced such documents myself. Particularly as denominational liturgies become more ample, it is less and less necessary to supplement them with other material. Too often of late I have been in services in which the worshiper was expected to use a basic hymn book, several supplementary hymnals, a separate liturgy book, and a multi-page bulletin; having only two hands, I have been tempted to put the bulletin between my teeth! I suspect this situation has developed because we who plan these services have spent so many years becoming adept at writing research papers, with books and notes spread all around us. So it does not occur to us that most worshipers only get distracted (and annoyed) when they are expected to use more than their hands can hold. Indeed, whenever possible, their hands should be free to be folded or uplifted in prayer.

14. Methodist readers do well to note the difference between the German pietistic tradition (which John Wesley knew and criticized for its separatism) and early Methodism. Methodism is often called too

casually a pietistic movement within the Church of England; this is in error if it implies separatist tendencies. First, Wesley urged his followers to attend the Anglican Church on every possible occasion, and he took care not to schedule Methodist meetings at conflicting hours. When Methodists were not practicing Anglicans, it was because they were made to feel unwelcome in Anglican parishes, not because they chose to live a separate existence. Second, Wesley did everything possible to counteract the notion that the Eucharist is the privilege of the select few. He urged regular reception by all serious seekers—even those who were uncertain of their salvation but earnestly yearned for it. (See, for example, his sermon entitled "On the Duty of Constant Communion.") In the eighteenth century nothing did as much as the Methodist movement to increase, not decrease, participation in the Eucharist in England.

15. See J. Ernest Rattenbury, *The Eucharistic Hymns of John and Charles Wesley*. Published originally in 1948 by Epworth Press, London, and then long out of print, this work has happily been reissued in 1990 by The Order of Saint Luke and is available from OSL Publications, 5246 Broadway, Cleveland, OH 44127-1500. Unfortunately, neither edition has an index of the 166 hymns by first lines; however, a separate index can be obtained upon request from OSL.

The book is more valuable for its hymn collection than for Rattenbury's commentary, which at times is not entirely accurate, particularly as to John Wesley's extract of Daniel Brevint's work, *The Christian Sacrament and Sacrifice*. In an unpublished paper, I have compared Brevint's original text (not included in Rattenbury) with Wesley's abridgement. The comparison shows, I believe, that at points Wesley actually intensified the theology of the eucharistic Presence by altering Brevint's text, whereas Rattenbury suggested that John diluted the Anglican theology of Brevint by shortening the original tract.

16. On the American scene, at least some of the deterioration of eucharistic piety can be traced to the otherwise commendable ecumenicity of the frontier camp meeting. There Methodists, Presbyterians, and Baptists encamped together for days at a time. The first two groups desired to have communion together. Baptists were less than enthusiastic—first, because they did not attach a high importance to communion and were accustomed to very few observances each year; and second, because many of them felt it to be a service of congregational covenant, not to be shared by others. (Even today some Baptists receive communion only within their own

local congregations, not even with other congregations of the same denomination.) Therefore, the Baptists typically left the campground early.

After the departure of the Baptists, the Methodists and Presbyterians observed the sacrament. But Presbyterians, schooled in close self-examination that often resulted in self-exclusion, did not all participate. From the Baptists, Methodists tended to get the idea that the Eucharist isn't really very important, and from the Presbyterians, Methodists got the notion that many are not worthy to receive. Both concepts were rejected by Wesley, yet afflicted later Methodists to a large degree.

Wesley also clearly rejected the infrequency of the Eucharist, such as practiced by Baptists and Presbyterians (as in Anglicanism in his own time). He reported in his journals receiving the sacrament himself two and three times per week. The American Methodist practice of having the sacrament once a quarter was a practical concession by Wesley and is in no way related to Zwingli's preference for communion four times a year.

The Methodist movement in the United States relied primarily upon lay preachers, and Wesley was not about to allow the unordained to celebrate the sacraments. Those who were ordained were used primarily as supervisory clergy (known in earlier times as "presiding elders" and later as "district superintendents"). It was the duty of these ordained clerics to visit four times each year the congregations over which they had jurisdiction, to conduct the church business in what was called a "quarterly conference" and to celebrate the sacraments. Unfortunately, when ordained clergy became more numerous and could function as resident pastors, the earlier pattern of quarterly communion continued, though the original rationale for it vanished. By then American Methodists had generally become so unfamiliar with their history that the much more frequent eucharists of the early Methodists in England were unknown to them.

17. Usually it is the Anglo-Catholic Oxford Movement (or Tractarianism) that is credited with the eucharistic renaissance in the Church of England. But note the careful research of Horton Davies in *Worship and Theology in England: Watts and Wesley to Maurice* (Princeton: Princeton University Press, 1961), 223-27.

Davies begins his discussion with this assertion:

> In the light of the sacramental and ecclesiological emphases of the Oxford Movement, it is customary but nonetheless erroneous to suppose that the Evangelicals, in appreciating the pulpit, depreciated the Sacraments. So far

> is this from the truth that the Evangelicals can rightly be claimed as pioneers in restoring the Sacrament of Holy Communion to its central place in the Anglican cultus. (p. 223)

This Davies goes on to connect with Wesley's "high conception of the Sacrament of the Eucharist."

## 5. TOWARD A RENEWAL OF EUCHARISTIC UNDERSTANDING

1. The term *host* here alludes to Christ as the One who provides table hospitality. The word is derived from the Latin root *hostis,* which originally meant "stranger," but came in time to mean one who graciously entertained a stranger or other guest.

To complicate matters, however, there is an entirely separate use of the term *host* in eucharistic parlance, particularly within the Roman Catholic tradition. This second use is derived from a different Latin root, *hostia,* meaning an animal sacrifice. In this sense, "Christ the Host" is tied to the medieval understanding of the representation of the sacrifice of Christ as the Lamb of God upon the altar of the church. Because this sacrificial offering of Christ was centered in the eucharistic bread, in this tradition the communion wafer is itself often referred to as "the Host."

It is unfortunate that in English *hostis* and *hostia* both came to have the same form. To avoid confusion, in this book the term *host* is used only in the first sense and should be taken to mean the gracious hospitality of God toward us.

2. In the Eastern liturgy two important ceremonial actions are used, neither of which could now be readily imported to the West without introducing a high degree of artificiality, but they indicate the importance of the Spirit to the Eucharist. (1) Hot water, called *zeon,* is added to the wine as a sign of the fire of the Spirit. (2) The eucharistic elements are fanned with a cloth as a sign of the breath or wind of the Spirit.

3. In *Baptism: Christ's Act in the Church,* I have discussed more fully the nature of signs, distinguishing between "signs" and "symbols" based on the way these words are used in popular speech. (See entries in the index on p. 207 of that book.) I have not here repeated those discussions, but the clothing in the store window would fall into the category of "symbol," while the clothing treasured by the bereaved parents would be "signs."

4. A kind of permission to view the Eucharist as an act of personal penitence and devotion entered the liturgy by the side door during the Middle Ages. Early in that period, the priest, while vesting in the sacristy, said assigned prayers about his utter unworthiness to serve at the altar. That finished, he went into what had originally always been a congregational service. But as time progressed and the call for Masses for the dead increased, the sacristies could not hold all of the vesting priests who needed to say Mass before breakfast. Hence it became the custom that prior to Mass the vestments of the priest were placed on the altar itself. There he robed, saying his penitential prayers, and then proceeded directly into the liturgy (with little or no congregation present on most occasions).

Later clergy, not knowing the origin and early location of their vesting prayers, took it for granted that the Eucharist properly begins with private penitential acts. Protestants, with their sturdy (if often misunderstood) doctrine of the priesthood of all believers, readily expanded the opening penitential prayers to include all present. Thus what the priest once did in private before the service, the whole congregation came to do in public at the beginning of the liturgy. Later this was given a presumably historical and theological defense by appealing to the order of events in Isaiah 6:1-8, in which cleansing from personal sin precedes instruction and commitment. Isaiah, however, was not dealing with corporate worship at all, let alone the liturgy of the Christian church; and there is no evidence that the Isaiah passage was ever seen as a pattern for the eucharistic rite prior to the developments just described.

5. From the final stanza of Horatio Bonar's hymn text "Here, O my Lord, I see thee face to face," written in 1857 and inspired by the Revelation 19:6-9.

## 6. CONDUCTING THE EUCHARIST

1. In such cases an abbreviated sermon often has been given a different name, such as "meditation" or—heaven help us—"sermonette." ("Sermonettes are for Christianettes," Paul Scherer used to observe wryly.) Since Vatican II, Protestants have taken to calling abbreviated sermons "homilies," on the mistaken assumption that what distinguishes the two terms is length. In fact, neither "sermon" nor "homily" implies anything directly about how long the preacher speaks. *Sermon* is derived from a Latin term, *sermo* ("discourse,"

"learned talk") and *homily* from a Greek term, *homilia* ("a speech," "communication with a group of persons"). The fact that the two terms are largely interchangeable is evidenced by the traditional habit of calling the study of sermon construction "homiletics" rather than "sermonics."

The real difference in the terms in Roman Catholic understanding arose from recent historical circumstances. Before Vatican II, the priest's Sunday morning remarks were called a sermon; often these were loosely attached to a biblical text, if at all. Vatican II insisted that the preacher's remarks should instead be the exposition of biblical material, especially that of the revised lectionary. As a way of signaling to priests the fact that something different was now being expected of them in the pulpit, it was deemed wise to switch from the familiar Latin term to the lesser-used Greek term.

Since Roman Catholic priests tend to be more concise in the pulpit than their Protestant counterparts, it came to be assumed (on both sides of the fence) that a homily is a short sermon. In fact, in Catholic parlance, a homily is what Protestants traditionally call "expository" or "textual" preaching, while a sermon is what Protestants dub "topical" preaching. Protestant preachers do well to continue to call their preaching "sermons," whether seven minutes, seventeen minutes, or seventy minutes in length.

2. Among those who trace their origin to the Wesleyan movement, it has been common practice to have worshipers move forward in groups suitable to the length of the church's communion rail. All kneel at the same time and, after all have received the eucharistic elements, all are dismissed at the same time. Some clergy, rather than saying simply, "Arise, and go in peace," launch into rather extended exhortations of one kind or another at each dismissal, thus in aggregate consuming an undue amount of time if a large number of "tables" is needed to serve the entire congregation.

3. It should be noted that while in some traditions the use of one of the creeds of the church is specified for each Sunday, a carefully constructed eucharistic prayer recites the work of God in much the same way as a good creedal statement. Therefore, it can well be argued that a creed is optional when the Eucharist is celebrated, but that when not celebrated the creed can help to supply what is missing.

The mandated use of a creed on Sunday is a late development. It appears to have been introduced first in 473 when the formula hammered out at the Councils of Nicaea and Constantinople in 325 and 381 respectively was introduced at Antioch to combat the Arian heresy. Such use was not accepted in Rome for more than half a millennium, and then primarily because in 1014 Pope Benedict VIII submitted to political pressure from Emperor Henry II. Another half millennium later, many Protestants opted to use the Apostles' Creed on Sundays rather than the later and longer Nicene Creed, though the Apostles' Creed had its origins in baptismal rites, not weekly worship.

4. This text is one of a number of common liturgical texts used by Protestants and Catholics across the English-speaking world under the aegis of ICET (International Consultation on English Texts). Note well that in the *Benedictus* "he" refers to Christ, not the worshiper. Hence, if changed in the interest of inclusiveness it should be altered to "Blessed is the One who comes," not to "Blessed are those who come." The theological intimation is that as Jesus entered Jerusalem humbly on a donkey when acclaimed by the crowd, so in the Eucharist Christ approaches in the humble forms of bread and wine when we proclaim the work and benefits of salvation.

5. Particularly in the Calvinistic tradition, often the pouring of the wine is a part of the third great action, not the first. At the offering, the elements are simply placed on the table or uncovered. Only following the eucharistic prayer is the wine poured, immediately after the bread is broken. While this has certain merits, it also can engender awkwardness. During the eucharistic prayer, at the words of institution, it is appropriate for the celebrant to hold the elements before the congregation. But a flagon can be large, heavy, and difficult to present gracefully in such a manner; even when it is not, the presentation of a pitcher does not connote drinking in the same way as does the presentation of a cup. And certainly the celebrant should not hold up an empty chalice. Hence, it is best to pour the wine before the eucharistic prayer, unless the acts of lifting the vessels within the prayer is deemed undesirable.

6. On several occasions I have seen well-intended attempts to combine this offering with liturgical dance; in every instance the presentation of bread and wine by dancers has been more dramatic than placing food on a table deserves to be. The taking of the bread and wine is, after all, an introductory act. When this action causes more comment than the three actions that follow, the cart has been put before the proverbial horse.

7. This posture is shown in catacomb drawings. It should be gracious and inviting, as if reaching out to embrace both God and the people. I tell my students that they are most apt to attain an appropriate stance by imagining that someone is standing about fifteen feet in front of

them, ready to toss a beach ball their way. Hence they have dubbed this "the invisible beach ball technique."

8. In many older rites, there was no place indicated for breaking of the bread as a separate action; hence, the bread came to be broken during the institution narrative. Happily that practice can now be discontinued, as the breaking becomes its own action after the eucharistic prayer is concluded.

It is advisable to lift the chalice and loaf and to replace them on the table between sentences in the rite, not mid-sentence. Otherwise the manual actions are likely to be awkward, the reading is apt to be jerky, or both.

For reasons that are obscure, throughout the English-speaking world and across denominational lines, it has become routine for many celebrants to say "Take; eat" as if it were a hyphenated word of two syllables: "Take-eat." Those who cannot break the habit do well to alter the text to read, "Take and eat." Indeed, despite a lack of grammatical warrant in any of the New Testament passages, the *Lutheran Book of Worship* of 1978 rendered it in precisely this way, thus avoiding the annoying problem.

9. During the Reformation period and into the Colonial era in America, Calvinists erected long tables and benches on communion occasions, to which worshipers went during the distribution. The practice is worthy of being reinstituted, though worship spaces with fixed pews and narrow aisles do not readily lend themselves to such reform. Where the reintroduction of this practice is contemplated, let it be clearly understood that there is to be no attempt to replicate the upper room meal, such that the table is designed to seat exactly twelve persons. Such slavish following of New Testament upper room narrative prevents us from seeing the full range of antecedents to the eucharistic feast—from the two guests at Emmaus, to the entire household of heaven in the Great Supper of the Lamb.

10. For a pertinent discussion of this issue by an African Roman Catholic, see Jean-Marc Ela's *African Cry* (Maryknoll, N.Y.: Orbis Books, 1986), translated from the French by Robert R. Barr, pp. 1-8. Ela argues for the use of millet bread and nut beer among the Kirdi people of Africa for whom these are staples, and for whom wheat bread and grape wine are both exotic and expensive. The traditional elements, he contends, cause the Eucharist to be "rendered meaningless"; for "the symbolism of the Eucharist escapes the savanna people or the forest people because the meaning of wheat bread and grape wine in European culture escapes them" (p. 5).

11. Instead of resting on the table, a candle atop a long standard may be placed on either side in sockets or holders at floor level; such candles can also be carried in procession where the custom of using processional torches is observed.

In traditional practice two candles on or at the table are lighted only on eucharistic occasions, and thus are called "eucharistic lights." Other candles may be found on the wall behind the table. These, called "office lights" (often six in number), are lighted for other services. Those Protestants who have only recently begun to use candles in church frequently place two on the table and light them at every service—thereby confusing visitors accustomed to the more traditional practice if they visit on a noneucharistic occasion.

Often symbolism is imposed on the eucharistic lights. They are said to represent the two natures of Christ, or the church militant and the church triumphant, or the two Testaments of Scripture, or this world and the next, and so on. In truth, centuries ago churches were very dark, particularly those whose windows were filled by stained glass. In order to read from the service book, the priest needed illumination. One candle placed at each end of the altar supplied sufficient light while creating a minimum of shadows. Only later did people invent theological reasons for using these two candles.

12. As implied in the previous note, we do well to be suspicious of imposed symbolism. Clearly the chief function of the fair linen is to cover the table, in accordance with the custom that a good banquet calls for a good tablecloth; no secondary justification is needed. It can be argued that seeing the fair linen as Jesus' unneeded shroud is on the same level as building a Lord's Table to look like a sarcophagus to remind us that Jesus no longer needs a tomb. The difficulty is that human beings seem inclined (if not actually determined) to read symbolic meanings into their significant experiences. Given that fact, I think the fair-linen-as-unneeded-shroud has a tad more validity and appeal (to say nothing of fiscal practicality) than the massive-stone-table-as-empty-tomb.

13. A coherent aesthetic program implies careful policy-making and planning at the local level under competent artistic guidance. Particularly since liturgical items often are given as memorial gifts, without such oversight a hodge-podge effect is inevitable, for each donor can impose a personal preference in style with little thought to overall coherence. Sometimes such personal selections will even be totally inappropriate—and almost impossible to refuse once they have been made, or to retire gracefully at some future time.

Furthermore, those who oversee the selection need to guard against the kind of eclecticism that can creep into a democratic process when an attempt is made to please everyone through the typical I-will-let-you-have-this-if-you-will-let-me-have-that kind of compromise. One hesitates to say that artists should be given autocratic powers, but democracy is best served through the careful selection of artists who are then to be trusted, rather than through attempts to dictate or revise the judgments of those artists once they have been commissioned.

14. For a fuller consideration of the issue of baptized children as communicants, see my *Baptism: Christ's Act in the Church* (Nashville: Abingdon Press, 1982), pp. 82-83, 124-25, 189.

## 7. "THAT MY HOUSE MAY BE FILLED"

1. *The First Apology of Justin Martyr,* section 67. Cited here as in Bard Thompson's *Liturgies of the Western Church* (New York: World Publishing Co., 1961), 9.

2. The exclusion of women from the clergy often has more to do with cultural habits than theological proscriptions. Still, the theological reason sometimes given for the exclusion needs to be understood in order that its germ of truth can be retained and reinterpreted. That truth is that the person who presides at the Lord's Table, by the very action of doing what Jesus did, comes to represent Christ to the congregation. This is an inescapable reality as surely for Protestants who wish to deny it as for Catholics or the Orthodox who insist upon it; for Christianity is at heart an incarnational faith.

Those who oppose the ordination of women insist that a female cannot represent Jesus, since historically he was a male. But the other side can insist with equal logic that the question has to do not with representation as such, but with what is to be thus represented. Must the presider represent the historic maleness of Jesus? If so, why not also the historic Jewishness of Jesus, in which case no Gentiles could be ordained? Or is it the humanity of Christ, present within our midst, that is to be represented? If the latter, males and females are capable of representing the Host equally effectively—and equally inadequately.

## APPENDIX 2. THE EUCHARIST IN METHODISM

1. Sermon CI in collections of Wesley's works; for this sermon together with a helpful introduction, see *John Wesley,* edited by Albert

C. Outler in the series A Library of Protestant Thought series (New York: Oxford University Press, 1964), pp. 332-44.

2. James H. Rigg, *The Churchmanship of John Wesley* (London: Hayman Brothers and Lilly, 1878), pp 45, 59.

3. The Works of John Wesley, vol. 19: *Journal and Diaries,* edited by W. Reginald Ward and Richard P. Heitzenrater (Nashville: Abingdon Press, 1990). The London diary here cited ends on August 8, 1741. For the period (1743–1754) covered in the subsequent vol. 20 (the most recently published) there is no corresponding diary.

4. William R. Crockett, *Eucharist: Symbol of Transformation* (New York: Pueblo Publishing Company, 1989), p. 199. On the crowds attracted to Methodist Eucharists (ever under the auspices of Anglican priests, since Wesley was at pains not to be seen as a separatist), see pages 2-3 of J. Ernest Rattenbury's *The Eucharist Hymns of John and Charles Wesley* (Cleveland: OSL Publications, 1990). In his assessment in *Reasonable Enthusiast: John Wesley and the Rise of Methodism* (Philadelphia: Trinity Press International, 1989), Henry D. Rack is less inclined than other recent writers to make such claims for a eucharistic revival, at least in terms of frequency of reception; see particularly pp 416-19.

5. Hymn, "Jesu, my Lord and God, bestow," no. 66 in the 1745 collection. Note the allusion to the post-resurrection appearance of Jesus to Thomas in the address "My Lord and God" (cf. John 20:28)

6. These are the four Wesley eucharistic texts contained in *The United Methodist Hymnal* (Nashville: The United Methodist Publishing House, 1989). Their inclusion makes them widely accessible but should not be taken to mean these are the finest or the desirable number out of the Wesleyan corpus; these are simply the only four the majority of a particular revision committee could be persuaded to use. Hymnals of other Methodist denominations contains a wider variety of texts, particularly the British Methodist book *Hymns and Psalms* (London: Methodist Publishing House, 1983).

Editorial changes in *The United Methodist Hymnal* have largely to do with stylistic matters—the updating of Wesley's spelling, punctuation, and his use of italics and capitalizations. Several alterations were made, however, to render acceptable masculine language that is no longer understood generically. In the second hymn listed here "for God hath bid all humankind" originally read "for God hath bidden all mankind." In the first stanza of the fourth hymn "into us" originally read "into man"; other alterations in this hymn are cited in the next note.

7. Stanza 2 has been altered at two points for the sake of clear understanding. Line 1 originally read, "How can heavenly spirits rise."

Since Wesley's time "heavenly" has ceased to be used as an adverb; thus to the contemporary mind "heavenly spirits" suggests angels rather than people. Therefore the line was made to read "How can spirits heavenward rise."

Line 6 originally read: "Him that did the means ordain." Since the allusion "Father's Wisdom" may not be recognized as referring to Christ, "him" was changed to make the meaning explicit. Note that Wesley did capitalize "Wisdom," as has been done here; early printings of *UMH,* at least, place the initial letter in lower case, thus also obscuring the fact that "Father's Wisdom" is the person of Christ, not an abstract category.

8. At the English Reformation, Archbishop Cranmer corresponded with Calvin and unsuccessfully pleaded with Luther's associate, Melanchthon, to move to England. Martin Bucer, who had studied the teachings of both Luther and Zwingli and was an associate of Calvin's in Strassburg, did come to teach at Cambridge. His associate, Peter Martyr, taught at Oxford. Thus the English Reformation was an amalgam of continental developments. See Horton Davies's discussion on the early Anglican eucharistic controversy, chapter 3 of *Worship and Theology in England (I): From Cranmer to Hook, 1543–1603* (Princeton, N.J.: Princeton University Press, 1970).

Many Methodists wrongly suppose that the Wesleys were at odds with Calvinism on all points. In fact, the differences centered on the issues at the Synod of Dort (1619), known popularly by the mnemonic acrostic "TULIP":

Total depravity
Unconditional election
Limited atonement
Irresistible grace
Perseverance of the saints

Contention on these five points did not preclude agreement between the Wesleys and the Calvinists on liturgical theology.

9. John Calvin, *Institutes of the Christian Religion,* IV.XVII.32.

10. Geoffrey Wainwright, *Eucharist and Eschatology,* 2nd ed. (London: Epworth Press, 1978), pp. 134-35.

11. Letter of September 10, 1784, to Thomas Coke and Francis Asbury. See *John Wesley's Sunday Service of the Methodists in North America* (Nashville: United Methodist Publishing House, issue of *Methodist Review,* 1984), page ii following page 38.

12. Cited by Henry Rack, *Reasonable Enthusiast* (p. 418) from Frank Baker's *William Grimshaw* (London: Epworth Press, 1963), p. 152.

# FOR FURTHER READING

The amount of literature available on the Eucharist is daunting to anyone who is not a full-time scholar of the liturgy. The intimidating nature of the quest for further knowledge may be lessened by a brief, annotated bibliography. So small a collection cannot be comprehensive, but many of these books contain helpful bibliographical sections for yet more extensive study.

A number of books written a quarter of a century ago or more lay the foundations for what has been explored recently.

C.F.D. Moule's *Worship in the New Testament* (Richmond: John Knox Press, 1961) provides in chapter 2 a concise discussion of the Christian fellowship meal in relatively non-technical terms. (No. 9 in the Ecumenical Studies series of John Knox Press, Richmond, 1961.)

A fuller examination, with particular attention to the sacramentality of the Fourth Gospel is provided in Oscar Cullmann's *Early Christian Worship,* translated by A. Stewart Todd and James B. Torrance (Philadelphia: Westminster Press, 1953). Pages 11-19 provide a helpful distillation of Cullmann's argument.

Cullmann's understanding of the Eucharist is set forth briefly but a bit more broadly with reference to New Testament literature in a work he wrote together with F. J. Leenhardt: *Essays on the Lord Supper,* translated by J. G. Davies (Ecumenical Studies in Worship No. 1 of John Knox Press, Richmond, 1958). Leenhardt's theological study comprises the larger section of the book and clearly delineates doctrinal issues from a reformed perspective.

Two Jesuits provided crucial background from the Roman Catholic vantage point. Jean Daniélou, SJ, detailed typological interpretations of the Old Testament in *The Bible and the Liturgy* (No. III in the Liturgical Studies series of the University of Notre Dame Press, 1956). Chapters 8–11 are particularly pertinent (Daniélou followed the Vulgate numbering of the Psalms; hence what is called "Psalm XXII" in chapter 11 is known by all Protestants and most contemporary Roman Catholics as Psalm 23.)

A historical, rather than exegetical, approach was taken by Josef A. Jungmann, SJ, in *The Early Liturgy* (Notre Dame: University of Notre Dame Press, 1959, Liturgical Studies series no. VI). This study of the development of the Roman Rite up to the time of Pope Gregory the Great at the end of the sixth century is thorough and somewhat technical but neither boring nor mystifying.

A more detailed and technical examination, with particular emphasis on the indebtedness of eucharistic rites to synagogue prayer is Louis Bouyer's *Eucharist: Theology and Spirituality of the Eucharistic Prayer,* translated by Charles Underhill Quinn (Notre Dame: University of Notre Dame Press, 1968). Although heavy reading, the work contains portions of significant liturgical texts, Eastern and Western (both Catholic and Protestant).

*The Eucharistic Memorial,* the two-volume work of Max Thurian of the Taizé community in France, helpfully combines historical study with theological reflection. The volumes were translated by J. G. Davies and published by John Knox Press of Richmond in 1960 and 1961 respectively as numbers 7 and 8 of the Ecumenical Studies in Worship series. Part I gives Old Testament background, and Part II treats development within the church. Thurian was particularly concerned to interpret the sacrificial aspects of the Eucharist in ways that are neither locked into medieval categories nor repugnant to later understanding.

Undergirding all of the above is the giant of the twentieth century: Dom Gregory Dix's *The Shape of the Liturgy,* in which an Anglican Benedictine demonstrated the classical form of

Synaxis and fourfold Eucharist across the centuries (London: Dacre Press, 1945). Despite its ponderous style and massive size (764 pages), this benchmark work cannot be neglected. However, Dix's characterization of Zwinglianism as a doctrine of the real absence of Christ in the Eucharist is more clever than helpful for ecumenical dialogue; nor is his understanding of Calvin to be trusted.

Further back into our century, from the pen of another English cleric, this one a Congregationalist, comes P. T. Forsyth's *The Church and the Sacraments* (London: Independent Press, Ltd., 1917). Chapters VII, VIII, XII–XIV were far ahead of their time. Indeed, Forsyth saw the link between sacraments and ecclesiology with a clarity possibly unequalled by any writer since. The style is heavy Victorian prose; the content is worth it.

On the lighter side, in *At All Times and in All Places* (New York: The Seabury Press, 1965; rev. 3rd ed.) Massey H. Shepherd, Jr., gave imaginative glimpses of the way the Eucharist was celebrated in the years 150, 500, and 1400, and under Anglicanism in 1665 and 1830. Then in a manner to which many congregations have not caught up a quarter of a century later, he proleptically described what a celebration in 1970 should look like. This popularization of the development of the Eucharist is so engaging that the liberties the author takes in filling in some of the historical blanks are easily forgiven. A dozen plates helpfully illustrate the brief work (less than a hundred pages).

Two volumes provide mainstream eucharistic texts. Bard Thompson's *Liturgies of the Western Church* (New York: World Publishing Company, 1961) gives the narrative of Justin Martyr and the rites of Hippolytus, the medieval Mass, Luther, Zwingli, Bucer, Calvin, Cranmer, Knox, the English Puritans of Middleburg, the Westminster Directory, Baxter, and John Wesley. Each is prefaced with a very helpful commentary.

More readily available these days is *Prayers of the Eucharist: Early and Reformed*, edited by R. C. D. Jasper and G. J. Cuming (2nd ed. New York: Oxford University Press, 1980). This work covers more ground than Thompson, and its thirty-six entries are not limited to the Western church, but its very brief introductory paragraphs to each rite are meager by comparison.

A plethora of other books produced within the past quarter century provide much help. A good overview is provided in *The Study of Liturgy*, edited by Cheslyn Jones, Geoffrey Wainwright, and Edward Yarnold, SJ (New York: Oxford University Press, 1978). Section III contains fifteen articles on the Eucharist, and pertinent references occur elsewhere in the volume.

More recently *The New Dictionary of Sacramental Worship*, edited by Peter E. Fink, SJ (Collegeville, Minn.: The Liturgical Press, 1990) contains a wealth of information. In particular check its topical index under "Eucharist."

I. Howard Marshall has provided a summary of recent New Testament scholarship in *Last Supper and Lord's Supper* (Grand Rapids: William B. Eerdmans, 1980). The four tables at the end of the book do much to demystify Jewish Passover background, development of New Testament traditions, and the convoluted problem of competing paschal calendars.

*The Eucharist of the Early Christians,* translated by Matthew J. O'Connell (New York: Pueblo Publishing Company, 1978), provides ten essays by Willy Rordorf and others assessing the reports and theological expositions of the *Didache,* Clement of Rome, Ignatius, Justin, Irenaeus, Clement of Alexandria, Tertullian, Cyprian, Origen, and the *Didascalia* and *Apostolic Constitutions.*

From the Orthodox perspective comes the wonderful exposition of Alexander Schmemann, *For the Life of the World* (Crestwood, N.Y.: St. Vladimir's Seminary Press, 1973, expanded edition). Chapters 1 and 2, together with two appended articles, set forth the rich Orthodox understanding of liturgical theology—and may induce you to look also at Father Schememann's *Introduction to Liturgical Theology* (SVSP, 1966).

The title of *Eucharist and Eschatology* sets forth a crucial linkage too often overlooked in the past (London: Epworth Press, 1971). Geoffrey Wainwright combines biblical themes with ecumenical concerns. While I do not advocate reading the last pages of a mystery novel first, you may want to begin this book with its eight-page conclusion.

In *Eucharist: Symbol of Transformation,* William R. Crockett is concerned both with historical-theological development and with the relationship to the sacrament of contemporary issues of justice (New York: Pueblo Publishing Company, 1989). Its final chapter, "Contemporary Prespectives," is worth the price of the book.

More focused on one particular aspect of justice is Monika A. Hellwig's *The Eucharist and the Hunger of the World* (New York: Paulist Press, 1976). Its value is far out of proportion to its small size; unfortunately, in the interim since publication, the global problems discussed by Hellwig have intensified, not abated.

Global and ethnic perspectives on the Eucharist are provided in other ways by works such as *The Sacraments Today* by the South American Jesuit Juan Luis Segundo (Maryknoll, N.Y.: Orbis Books, 1974), translated by John Drury. While many issues discussed are of particular interest to Roman Catholics, the work is written with great clarity. Questions in an appendix facilitate group discussions of the issues.

*The Eucharist and Human Liberation* by Tissa Balasuria (Maryknoll, N.Y.: Orbis Books, 1979) provides an Asian liberationist perspective, again from a Roman Catholic background.

Although not directed specifically at eucharistic concerns, José Míguez Bonino's *Doing Theology in a Revolutionary Situation* (Philadelphia: Fortress Press, 1975) provides useful theological undergirding, particularly in the area of ecclesiology. Much the same can be said with respect to James Cone's *A Black Theology of Liberation* (Philadelphia: J. G. Lippincott Company, 1970).

Feminist perspectives on the Eucharist are found in Marjorie Procter-Smith's *In Her Own Rite* (Nashville: Abingdon Press, 1990), particularly chapter 6 and in more scattered ways in Marianne Sawicki's *Faith and Sexism* (New York: Seabury Press, 1979).

Books that deal concretely yet broadly on actual contemporary eucharistic celebration are far rarer than historical and theological treatments. Among the many values of James F. White's *Sacraments as God's Self Giving* (Nashville: Abingdon Press, 1983) are its proposals for reform, specifically items 12-20 of chapter 6. The book deals comprehensively with the seven historic sacraments and devotes the whole of chapter 3 to the Eucharist.

Culminating all is the small but crucial section on the Eucharist in the World Council of Churches Faith and Order Paper No. 111: *Baptism, Eucharist, and Ministry.* Designed for denominational discussion and congregational study, in fewer than eight pages this work brings into focus the contemporary impact of the historical debates and divisions and makes very concrete proposals for further dialogue.

# INDEX OF BIBLICAL TEXTS

# INDEX OF SUBJECTS